# Who Needs The Family?

*Also in this series of*
*London Lectures in Contemporary Christianity*

CHRISTIANS AND MARXISTS
by José Miguez Bonino

ISSUES OF LIFE AND DEATH
by Norman Anderson

CHRIST AND THE MEDIA
by Malcolm Muggeridge

HUMAN SCIENCE AND HUMAN DIGNITY
by Donald M. MacKay

# Who Needs The Family?

## A survey and a Christian assessment

### O. R. JOHNSTON

HODDER AND STOUGHTON
LONDON SYDNEY AUCKLAND TORONTO

*The author and publishers are grateful
to Gerald Duckworth & Co. Ltd. for permission
to reproduce lines from* Cautionary Verses *by Hilaire Belloc.*

British Library Cataloguing in Publication Data
Johnston, Olaf Raymond
    Who needs the family?. – (London lectures in
contemporary Christianity).
    1. Family
    I. Title    II. Series
    261.8'34'21      BV4526.2

ISBN 0 340 23986 7

First published 1979

Printed in Great Britain for
Hodder and Stoughton Limited,
Mill Road, Dunton Green, Sevenoaks, Kent
by Lowe and Brydone Printers Limited
Thetford, Norfolk

# TO
# PEGGY

# Contents

# Contents

# Foreword

This book represents the substance of the London Lectures in Contemporary Christianity, delivered at All Souls' Langham Place in April and May 1978. When the Trustees invited me to deliver these lectures they did me a great honour, and I felt that with my own background in the multi-disciplinary world of educational studies and Christian social thinking I could not refuse. In the event, time for preparation had to be snatched from an over-crowded life, and I am conscious that what follows is more of an introductory over-view of the territory rather than a detailed map. Yet such surveys have their own special value, especially if they can indicate – as I hope I have done – the creative points where the eternal truths of revealed Christian theology meet both the models and empirical data of academic researchers and the complex and pressing problems of living in the contemporary world.

It is also my conviction that corporatism (like internationalism) is fundamentally hostile to human dignity and diversity as well as a social objective against which the Christian mind, theologically equipped, will vigorously react. A strong family structure (like a healthy national life) is a source of individual identity and social vitality which urgently needs positive nurture today. If this book aids understanding and contributes to a new vision of our Christian calling in family, church and society, I shall be content.

The printed version of my lectures has profited much from the contributors to the discussion after each session, and from the perceptive comments of Miss Joyce Guy on the first draft. But I alone take responsibility for all the opinions expressed.

Raymond Johnston

# CHAPTER ONE

# The Family Unit

"Il n'y a point de tableau plus charmant que celui de la famille" – There is no more delightful spectacle than the family – wrote Rousseau in his renowned and seminal educational treatise *Emile*, which appeared in 1762. But what kind of picture did Rousseau have in mind? Already by the mid-eighteenth century Montesquieu, the great French lawyer and political philosopher, had begun to open mens' eyes to other societies. By his comparative studies he had started the relentless march towards moral relativism, and towards what we now know as sociology. Consequently, we are very conscious – almost hyperconscious – of the relativity of everything. We live in our global village with a wide diversity of cultures, of standards, of dress, of language, of morals.

There is some irony in this awareness at the very time when the homogeneous pattern of Western industrial civilisation is spreading so rapidly to the developing world. In these areas many other countries seemed destined to ape the developed patterns of Europe at the very time when we are trying to warn our own peoples against them, and what they bring with them – pollution, over-crowding, rootlessness, anonymity and alienation. Family relationships suffer from industrialisation, as we shall see, and in many ways anthropologists and others look with some envy at the family relations which they can still find in the non-industrialised parts of the world. Perhaps we might begin in our own country by recalling that it was Belloc in his *Moral Alphabet* who wrote:

F for the Family taking a walk
  In Arcadia Terrace, no doubt:
The parents indulge in intelligent talk,
  While the children they gambol about.

At a quarter-past six they return to their tea,
  Of a kind that would hardly be tempting to me,
  Though my appetite passes belief.
There is Jam, Ginger Beer, Buttered Toast,
  Marmalade,
With a Cold Leg of Mutton and Warm Lemonade,
And a large Pigeon Pie very skilfully made
  To consist almost wholly of Beef.

MORAL
A Respectable Family taking the air
  Is a subject on which I could dwell;
It contains all the morals that ever there were,
  And it sets an example as well.[1]

That of course is a cartoon of a certain brand of Victorian moralism; it echoes with a hollow unreality, with class consciousness, with artificiality – and it was meant to. But is it completely false? Are the days past when anyone could seriously assert that the family contains all the morals that ever there were, and it sets an example as well? Or are there still essential parts of our humanity which only the family can nourish – including moral awareness? Our aim is to see to what degree the serious principle behind Belloc's exaggerated jesting can still be said to be true, particularly in the light of the given certainties of the Christian Faith.

A reasonable sized book or a course of five lectures on family relationships cannot give the depth of coverage which a narrower area would permit. The enterprise presents several problems. There is a vast mass of data on the family – sociological, psychological, legal, historical, anthropological, literary and so on. Where shall we stop? Again, everyone is to some degree an expert (or feels themself to be an expert) because after all, most of us have had some family experience ourselves. Nearly all of us were born into a family and many of us have families of our own. Any writer or lecturer expounding Bunyan's theology, or Pascal's apologetic, or the imagery of T. S. Eliot, or the structure of *The Lord of the Rings*, might count on some initial open-mindedness and perhaps some respect; certainly audience or readers would come with fewer preconceptions. But because the family is the topic, there is a great temptation to feel we all know the answers almost before the questions are put.

We shall consider various varieties of family pattern, and examine the central tasks and functions of the family. After some remarks about the dynamics of family life and a brief glance at proposals to abolish the family, we shall finally attempt a critical appraisal of the "Western norm" of family life in the light of Christian teaching.

I

There are many varieties of family pattern. At first sight, when we extend our vision historically and geographically, we are presented with a bewildering variety. The basic question which the objective scientific student of family life asks is: "Who is conscious of being related to whom?" From the answers we discover what types of obligations arise.

One fascinating approach to this field is the purely anecdotal. If we comb the books of travellers, missionaries and explorers we can amass thousands of surprising statements. In some parts of Melanesia one inherits land on the mother's side and fruit trees on the father's side. In New Caledonia it is the maternal uncle who performs the ceremony of breathing life into the newborn child. The Korango and the Mesakin on the Nuba hills are quoted as commenting on their almost completely premarital sexual licence, "We are like goats."[2] But piling up such evidence, though it may be entertaining, only confuses the mind. We are seeking pattern and coherence. On further analysis anthropologists find various alternatives, various categories which they use to classify family life and family patterns. It may be useful to list in the abstract some of the broad varieties.

The sorts of category used by anthropologists are uncovered by questions like: Where will a newly-married couple live and bring up their family? Will they go to the home or the area of the wife, or of the husband? To use the technical term, is this culture characterised by the matrilocal family or the patrilocal family? Then we proceed to ask: How is descent reckoned? How is inheritance sponsored? Very often it is connected with the principal name taken by the married pair. Here we have the matrilineal pattern, where lineage and kindred is specified particularly through the mother, and the patrilineal, where it is the father that counts. Then there are questions about the foundation partners of families, e.g. whether one, or more than one spouse is permitted. More than one gives us a polygamous society. And then that type of community can be divided further into polyandrous and polygynous groups – polyandry meaning the wife can have more than one husband (which is extremely rare), and polygyny, which is the practice of having more than one wife (which is much more common). The alternative to the polygamous society is the monogamous society – where one man and one woman are supposed to undertake an exclusive loyalty to each other. But the biggest contrast of all is the one which we must examine more closely – that is, the very straight and crude contrast between primitive and modern. And by modern, perhaps with some insularity, I mean the family in modern western industrialised society, the family as most of us know it best.

Our most natural definition of the family in Britain today is "mum, dad and kids". This the anthropologist calls the *nuclear* family, the basic biological unit. To this central unit we sometimes add others in particular circumstances, after a little thought. But when we speak of *the* family in today's world, this is what we mostly mean. Other societies however include, quite naturally and normally, many other people.

For a start, grandparents one generation back are usually counted in. Often cousins, uncles, nieces are added; sometimes the sense of solidarity and kinship extends to a whole group, a whole clan, or a whole tribe, as happens in some primitive societies, where all those of one's father's generation are actually called "father". And the older men will call younger boys "son" irrespective of whether there is any actual blood relationship. This feeling of clan broadens the family consciousness and has many advantages, particularly in primitive conditions. It gives security and it makes the setting of norms and standards much more easy.

That does not mean however that in other societies apart from our own, the unique husband + wife + children group is not recognised. It certainly is. But we are asserting that there is a strongly-felt unity of a wider group. And this by contrast we therefore call the *extended* family; as distinct from the nuclear family. But urban living together with the decline of fixed and rigid social stratification have meant that extended family relationships are less frequent and less strongly felt in Britain (as in most Western industrial countries). The conditions of city life, occupational and social mobility assisted by rising educational standards and easy communications – all these have disturbed the settled pattern of life found in pre-industrial societies, and separated nuclear families from their wider kin and context.

Before moving on, we must note that the old theory of primitive promiscuity, developing through polygamy and then finally arriving at monogamy, is no longer accepted. The facts do not support this simplistic evolutionary hypothesis. Time and time again, the sociology and anthropology textbooks emphasise that every society known to us makes special provision for recognising the nuclear family. Even though the basic unit naturally attracts others to itself and lives in a wider context, yet the nuclear family is sensed as the basic building block; and steps are made to protect it and give it special privileges. And with privileges come special obligations.

## II

But what are the essential tasks of the family? Ultimately these stem from the constitution of humanity itself, and especially from the position of the infant child. There are basic needs of child-rearing and child-bearing which *must* be performed, otherwise humanity will perish. The human child is peculiarly helpless at birth, unlike many other living creatures. In comparison with other living things, the human child takes a long time to mature. The human child is not instinctually programmed. For example he does not know immediately at birth how to build a home, to use tools, to till the land, and so on. Admittedly the human child has a complex brain and immense creative potential. But all the skills of living and surviving are *taught*. These things are transmitted by cultural channels. The child needs to learn them. He does not "know" from birth. It is these essential needs of the child upon which the survival of the race depend, and which bring the importance of the family to the foreground.

In traditional pre-industrial societies the family was a type of microcosm, undertaking itself most of the tasks which the family group needed to survive. It may be useful to list these functions as anthropologists and sociologists have analysed them. Firstly the family regulated sexual expression and satisfaction, thus preventing constant conflict, confusion and competition. Secondly, the family regulated the production of children, thus ensuring that the community continued. Thirdly the family socialised the children, transmitting the culture, and ensuring therefore that they became mature citizens at some point in the future, to enter fully into the productive and continuing life of the society. Fourthly, the family protected the children. This protective function was in most cases undertaken not only in relation to the children but also to their grandparents; the active adults in most societies have not only handed duties downwards to their children, but also upwards to their elderly parents. Fifthly, after protection comes simple economic division of labour. This is seen in the most primitive societies, whether they are hunting societies or gathering societies. It is the father who hunts or gathers and it is the mother who rears the children. And sixthly, the family provides other resources which we can lump together – health care, recreation, training for work, and initiating into religion and myth, lore and literature. All these tasks in earlier societies, and in most primitive societies today, were and are undertaken by the family for itself. Admittedly there was sometimes a certain degree of specialisation in addition. There was the priest for religion and the medicine man for health. But the family was a many-faceted operational group, rich in a variety of tasks it could shoulder for itself.

A broad generalisation is at once obvious: in the transition from primitive to modern "Western" types of society many of these functions have been institutionalised outside the home. We have witnessed the "stripping" of the family of many of its former reasons for existence, and the handing over of these tasks to other specialised agencies. Put very crudely: in modern societies, work itself (that is, economically profitable work, employment in order to exist) mostly goes on outside the home. Religion is left to the churches, or perhaps as a vestigial superstition, to the astrology columns of the magazines. Work training is provided by industry or by the state or by a specialised institution. Certainly it now only rarely occurs within the family. Wider cultural initiation is undertaken by the school, the college, the university and so on. As for recreation – it is often the state or the local authorities which must provide us with facilities for whatever it may be. Pure entertainment has its own mammoth production industry too. For health we look increasingly to the state to provide the services of the specialised medical personnel. For protection, whether internal or external, we rely on the state to furnish us with police, courts,

armies, navy, and so on. In this way the family has been
deprived of many of its earlier functions as we have
developed into the modern industrial society which we take
for granted in all its complexity.

It is still possible however to make the task of the family
appear as a manifold, variegated pattern of challenges,
opportunities and obligations. This kind of analysis can be
produced by the social psychologist, and indeed in a very
daunting form. Miss Joan Cooper, former Director of
Social Work for the D.H.S.S., has written:

A family home may be thought of as functioning effectively when it:

offers adequate shelter, space, food, income and the basic amenities
which enable the adults to perform their marital, child-rearing and
citizenship roles without incurring so much stress that anxiety
inhibits a confident and positive performance;

secures the physical care, safety and healthy development of
children either through its own resources or through the competent
use of specialised help and services;

acknowledges its task of socialising children, encouraging their
personal development and abilities, guiding their behaviour and interests and informing their attitudes and values;

offers the experience of warm, loving, intimate and consistently
dependable relationships;

assures the mother of support and understanding, particularly
during the early child-rearing period, and provides the child with a
male/father/husband model which continues to remain important
through adolescence;

offers children an experience (2–6 years) of group life, so extending
their social relationships, their awareness of others and intellectual
development;

responds to children's curiosity with affection and reasoned explanations, and respects children through all developmental stages as
persons in their own right, so securing affection and respect for
others within the family circle and wider social network;

co-operates with school, values educational and learning opportunities and encourages exploration and a widening of experience;

supports adolescents physically and emotionally while they are achieving relative independence of the family, personal identity, sexual maturity, a work role, relationships within society and the testing out of values and ideologies;

provides a fall-back supportive system for the young marrieds during their child-bearing period.[3]

And after reading such a catalogue it would not be surprising if most parents did not themselves feel the need for a fall-back supportive system! In fact the above provides a splendid description of the various things which the two-stage nuclear family can and ought to do in the subtler intangible field of consciousness, relationships and identity. We have moved from stressing physical and communal needs to an emphasis upon psychological, individual needs. Inner resources of mind and spirit are now called for. The perspective has shifted dramatically. And grandparents are quietly forgotten.

Such are the tasks of the family ancient and modern. But even in the modern "Western" family changes have taken place and are taking place in the way in which these tasks are performed – changes which even put in question the possibility of these tasks being performed at all. Many good things have happened which have assisted and enriched family life in Britain over the last fifty years. Smaller families has made more personal attention to children possible. Affluence has certainly made the surroundings of children more pleasant and increased the assistance upon which parents can call for help with home tasks. Rising health standards have made family life less of a strain and a tragedy. One huge difference between family life today and family life in the Victorian age lies in the fact that in the nineteenth century death was not simply a common-place thing, but the death of other *children*, one's own brothers and sisters, was a frequent occurrence. And higher educational standards have helped all of us to understand the needs of children. So here are possibilities for the improvement of the quality of home and family life.

But there are things on the other side, and in particular, the results of social and occupational mobility. This has meant the pulling up of family roots in the locality, where father has lived and possibly even several generations before him – where an extended kinship network always enabled the family to call upon well-known and trusted relatives in times of emergency. So the modern nuclear family in our society has fewer tasks to undertake than in earlier ages, but it has in many ways fewer personal and kinship resources from which to draw strength, help and cohesion. For example, the housewife who is not in employment and whose parents are dead, or live in another area, can be the loneliest of individuals today. She can come under tremendous tensions when she has small children, and there is no-one to call upon. She can feel a strange isolation too when the children are no longer at home. Betty Yorburg in her book *The Changing Family* writes as follows:

> At least some of the stresses that families experience in modern societies can be attributed to a lack of adequate substitutes for the services that the extended family performed in the past: care and support for the aged and incapacitated, child care and house-keeping help, and a built-in supply of wider social contacts, confidantes and companions in recreational activities.[4]

Certainly the nuclear family *alone* is a very small unit to bear the emotional weight which it is usually expected to carry. Larger and more extended families diffuse intense reactions and provide alternative models. Yet expectations were never higher – as the TV advertisements for breakfast cereals remind us! And this is only one of the strains today's families face.

Where then is the British family going? There are optimistic and pessimistic assessments. For an optimistic assessment we might instance Ronald Fletcher's book *The Family and Marriage in Britain Today*.[5] Fletcher skilfully attempts to show those who have a tendency to deal in gloom and doom from time to time, that their fears are unjustified. He does not believe that family life is disintegrating.

For pessimism however; there are other writers equally well qualified and equally sensitive. I think for example of Dr. Uri Bronfenbrenner, the American social psychologist who came over to speak at an important Government-sponsored symposium at All Souls' College, Oxford, on the family. In his outstanding paper he provided the following facts about American society. It is worth remembering that we largely share the cultural characteristics of the United States, whose influence on British life was never greater than today.

In 1971 forty-three per cent of the nation's mothers worked outside the home; in 1948 the figure was only eighteen per cent; one in every three mothers with children under six is working today;

as more mothers have gone to work, the number of other adults in the family who could care for the child has decreased; fifty years ago about half of all households included at least one other adult besides the parents; today the figure is below five per cent;

the divorce rate among families with children has been rising substantially during the last twenty years; the percentage of children from divorced families is almost double what it was a decade ago; if present rates continue, one child in six will lose a parent through divorce by the time he is eighteen;

in 1970 almost a quarter of all children were living in single-parent families; nearly double the rate for a decade ago; over the same period the number of families headed by women who have never been married has tripled; almost half the mothers who are single parents of children under six are now in the labour force, and a third of these are working full-time;

among families that are intact and well-off economically research results indicate that parents are spending less time in activity with their children.[6]

His main concern in this particular paper was the question: How much do parents and their children actually interact to the benefit of the youngsters, as distinct from simply being in the same house or room together? What happens when they are together? We may perhaps find part of the disturbing answer in one other sentence from his paper: "The average American family now consists of a mother, a father, two point four children, and at least one television set." In a work of this size it would not be right to attempt a simple answer to the question "Where is the British family going?", but with those two possibilities of optimism and pessimism in mind we turn to consider a related topic which gives an extra dimension to our understanding, and to which the above quotation forms a fitting introduction, namely, the internal dynamics of family life.

## III

The analysis of complex and intense emotional ties is a fascinating study. There are in fact eight possible dyadic relationships (i.e. one person to one other person) within the nuclear family, though in order to have experience of them all a family would need at least four children; two of each sex, as you will see. There is the husband/wife relationship, the father/son relationship, the father/daughter relationship, the mother/son relationship, the mother/daughter relationship, sister/sister, brother/brother, and brother to sister – eight possible dyadic relationships. Since any family begins as a tightly related group, all of these, where they exist, interact with each other and change. The family is a system, so change at one point will virtually always mean change at another point. Most of these changes will be unintentional and sometimes quite unexpected. If there is suffering or malfunction at any one point in the family, its effects will be felt elsewhere.

The theory and practice of psychiatry has opened up new worlds of subtlety in the analysis of human relationships. Before the rise of psychiatry in the early twentieth century, it was the drama and the novel which explored the family and family relationships through the creative imagination. From Sophocles through Shakespeare to Balzac or Galsworthy, writers felt the perennial attraction of infinite variety within the basic family pattern. Today however a new approach is with us, claiming the status of science and based originally on the data of human mental strain and disorder – the abnormal patients of Sigmund Freud.

The Freudian myths (the word "myth" is used here in no dismissive or derogatory sense; but as an explanatory picture) were based on extensive interviews and case-work analysis with disturbed individuals. And Freud came to recognise that family relations can be fraught with powerful instinctual loves and hates, envies and desires, whether to kill or to supplant, to engulf or to eat or to crush. Many of the often puzzling personality characteristics which define a particular adult are the result of unconsciously "remembered" experiences of the earliest months of life, psychic "wounding" (trauma) or jealousy or illicit longing to attack or to replace a parent. Much of the Freudian conceptual framework has stood the test of usefulness as an exploratory model, though it is not the whole story. The postulate of a universal Oedipus complex, for example, is well known and is certainly a key idea. In his book on Freud, David Stafford-Clark sums it up rather well in these words: "Everywhere men must be prevented from desiring their mothers and wishing to kill their fathers."[7] The uninitiated may smile, but this is an essential postulate of the Freudian analysis of what is going on within the family. It is disturbing and deeply pessimistic. But the Freudian picture has been immensely influential. And it does throw light on why and how family experiences can be so destructive, even to crippling some members for life.

Modern therapeutic approaches, however, pay more attention to the total family as a functioning unit, trying to become aware of what the family as a whole is doing to and for each of its members. Family therapists become skilled in identifying "scapegoats", "ambassadors", "messengers", and so on. Increasingly often such analysis is possible in the situation of family group therapy, where the whole family is seen and interviewed together. Practitioners in this field see two needs as paramount. The first is *communication*, so that throughout the family people can express themselves and understand each other. Thus the family can move and respond as an integrated whole. It can cohere and develop. Secondly, with communication must come *order*. In a fascinating article A. C. R. Skynner writes of the family as a system and a group. He moves on from communication to write as follows:

> The parts of the group, like the parts of the individual, are not all on one level but require to be arranged in a certain hierarchical order if they are to function effectively. No one disputes this in the organisation of the central nervous system, where lower centres are under the dominance of higher, or in the individual where more basic drives and instincts require to be subordinated to ego controls and these in turn to super-ego sanctions. But groups and families also have an optimum type of organisation which must involve a form of dominance hierarchy and while there is again a range of possibilities of varying effectiveness, it appears that breakdown of the authority structure – whether through the loss of control of a nation by its government, abdication of responsibility by a father, or destruction of the cortex through birth injury – leads to unco-ordinated release of tendencies which can be damaging to the whole system, however valuable these may be within proper bounds and in their proper place.[8]

This gives us the "feel" of the way in which the family therapist views the family as a total system.

But even with good communication and a stable hierarchy, time means change and every family changes as the months and the years go on. The system alters with each of the traditional crises. The arrival of a child – i.e. the pregnancy and birth events. These decisively modify family relationships. Next, the child beginning to speak; immediately verbal communication has an extra point of origin and reception within the family. The child going to school, when the parents lose the total grip that they have hitherto had upon their offspring; the child himself starts out on a new adventure. The next stage is when the child becomes adolescent, and subsequently the child becoming an adult and leaving home. Then comes a new phase with the young adult marrying and the original parents finding themselves as "in-laws". There follows the menopause, grandparenting, and finally of course, the death of a spouse. In addition we can consider the arrival of a second, third, fourth, fifth (etc.) child, the death of a child, divorce, lengthy illness and so on, which may or may not come the way of the family as it develops.

Much less favourable however in its attitude to the enrichment and success of the nuclear family (to which this section has been restricted) is the existential psychiatry movement. The Scottish prophet R. D. Laing, with his South African friend David Cooper (four years his junior) as his lieutenant, are psychiatrists who have made a considerable impact. In his earlier years Laing made some original and widely valued contributions to psychiatric thinking, but more recently he has come to view the family as a burden and a common cause of mental illness. These writers often strike a note of rather shrill protest. Their intellectual foundation is in fact very close to a new kind of anarchism. It makes a heady brew in today's rather unsettled religious and political climate.

Laing sees schizophrenia as a phenomenon which should be investigated in a social context. Not, that is, by the patient coming to the psychiatrist, but rather by the psychiatrist examining just exactly what the patient is in his environment. In particular, attention must be paid to what he is and what he means in the family context. The "mad" person (Laing always uses inverted commas) or the schizophrenic will often be a tension-conductor or a scapegoat. He or she bears this pressure so that the rest of the family can continue in some sort of equilibrium. Add the political stance and we get a message like this (from David Cooper's most recent book, *The Grammar of Living*):

> The bourgeois nuclear family (which in this context I shall henceforth refer to as "the family") is the principal mediating device that the capitalist ruling class uses to condition the individual, through primary socialisation, to fit into some *role complex* that suits the system (the family thus generates a conflict between the active reality of a person and the conditioned passivity of his role complex).[9]

A particular political rhetoric is echoed here as well as psychiatric analysis. The Laing–Cooper revolt is in essence a revolt against all rules, roles and relations, in favour of something known as "the real self", or the authentic person. This doctrine stands squarely in the tradition of Rousseau and the Romantics, and the more modern existentialist protest, which is their descendant. But such a posture is in fact a denial of human social responsibility. The weakness of Laing's prescriptions has been beautifully set out by Professor David Martin in the following elegant words:

> . . . one person's pursuit of authenticity is another person's blasted possibility. It only needs one such liberated spirit to leave a trail of other people's broken potentialities behind him.
>
> Over-development of the aspiration towards "the real" devalues the common, repeated, everyday in which the profoundest satisfaction can lie. Thus family life both breeds a sense of quiet desperation and suffocation *and* a common life of steady ritual, renewed confidence, demarcated privacies and deep familiarities without which people are lost souls. The familial is the familiar: that which defines, orders, and maintains the personal world. People can die within that order; they can barely live without it or without some substitute which is usually more, not less, restrictive. Moreover, many of the processes he describes are general phenomena of life operating as the necessary ground of social existence: for example partial reciprocity, focused and restricted identifications, unacknowledged systems of rules, proffered ranges of distinctions, definitions and options, processes of prescribing not by directions but by attributions and labels. These processes have their costs, which are sometimes heavy and repressive, but they admit an amelioration in the way they operate, and *total* reciprocity, *absolute* openness and lack of demarcation are neither possible nor desirable. All viable culture is a restriction on "world-openness", and that restriction in turn makes possible (though not inevitable) the recovery of some openness to the world.[10]

This is a fine analysis and a counter to the view of internal family dynamics as necessarily negative and destructive. Of course Laing identified family factors as a cause for concern – families turned sour *can* inflict lasting damage on their members. But this points to the need for family renewal, not to the disposability of the family.

## IV

Laing's gloomy picture brings us to a consideration of the advocates of the abolition of the family. Many thinkers since Plato in his *Republic* have played with the idea that it might be good or desirable to abolish the family completely. This has never been a greater temptation than in the context of some kind of Utopian political recipe. Undoubtedly the most powerful in modern times was that of Karl Marx. In their righteous indignation against the extremes of wealth and poverty in the nineteenth century, Marx and Engels certainly foresaw the disappearance of the family, even if they did not actually press for its abolition. In 1848 they wrote in the *Communist Manifesto*:

> Abolition of the family! Even the most radical flare up at this infamous proposal of the Communists.
>
> On what foundation is the present family, the bourgeois family, based? On capital, on private gain. In its completely developed form this family exists only among the bourgeoisie. But this state of things finds its complement in the enforced absence of the family among the proletarians, and in public prostitution.
>
> The bourgeois family will vanish as a matter of course when its complement vanishes, and both will vanish with the vanishing of capital. . . .
>
> The bourgeois claptrap about the family and education, about the hallowed relation of parent and child, becomes all the more disgusting, the more, by the action of modern industry, all family ties among the proletarians are torn asunder, and their children transformed into simple articles of commerce and instruments of labour.[11]

As we know from the story of the Industrial Revolution there is some truth in this kind of accusation. Industrialisation affects population distribution and housing, and hence human relationships. But it does not follow that the family itself is a bourgeois invention. Roughly thirty years later, Marx's collaborator Engels wrote in his book *The Origin of the Family, Private Property and the State*, these words:

> With the transformation of the means of production into collective property, the monogamous family ceases to be the economic unit of

society. The private household changes to a social industry. The care and education of children becomes a public matter. Society cares equally well for all children, legal or illegal.[12]

The implication is clear – there will be no need for the family.

Given this kind of theoretical background it was not un-expected that in the 1920s Soviet Russia, at that time the world's only state professing to organise its social life according to Marxist theory, should attempt to dissolve family ties completely. Accordingly, marriage became civil registration only, and that in a most undignified and hole-in-corner way. Divorce became possible by simple declaration. Incest, bigamy and adultery ceased to be criminal offences. Abortion on request was made possible without the necessity even to declare a reason, and a little later the labour laws made it obligatory for people to accept any post imposed on them, wherever that job might be. No modification was conceded even in the case of a husband posted away from his wife, or a wife sent to employment away from her husband. As a result of these policies family ties were weaker by 1930. But other effects were also noticed. By 1935 it was clear that the nation had been en-feebled and that it could not call upon such strong and wide-spread popular allegiance in the case of a possible war. The specific results of the anti-family policy were serious. Free divorce and abortion had pushed down the birth rate. In 1934 in the hospitals of Moscow there were 53,000 births and 154,000 abortions. Juvenile delinquency, violence in schools, vandalism, sadistic behaviour by quite young children – all these things had spread. The recognition dawned that so-called sexual liberation had put the weak and the shy at risk. It was the strong, the arrogant and the reckless that triumphed. Women were more oppressed than others.[13] So the party line was changed. From 1935 onwards the process was put in reverse, at any rate as far as the official ideology was concerned. Marriage became desirable and children were taught from their earliest years that it was a serious matter, a commitment for life. One article[14] records an interesting sign: in 1936 wedding rings re-appeared in the shops of Moscow. The easy dissolution of marriage ceased and divorce was made very difficult. Maternity was praised and abortion made hard to obtain. Respect for elders, especially parents, became a regular theme in the mass media. The lesson had been learned the hard way.

Another place where it is sometimes said the family has been abolished is in the Israeli agricultural collective group known as the kibbutz. The ideal is characterised by community living, common ownership of all property and the communal rearing of all children. Yet the studies[15] show even here that couples form lasting partnerships which are recognised by the kibbutz, so great is the desire for the security of one committed partner with whom to share one's intimate life – in both the physical and the psychological sense. Most children are planned, and though communally reared, children increasingly see more and more of their parents as they grow up. Most significantly, the terms "father", "mother", "son", "daughter" are used exclusively in precisely the same way as in the traditional family. Earlier kibbutz thought, at the start of the movement, was heavily weighted against any kind of private life. Even private radios and private kettles were banned. The main emphasis in life was work, demanded for sheer survival. We may well wonder how the members spent their free time. The literature suggests communal singing, folk dancing . . . and group discussion. But all this took place en masse. Any husband and wife in those early days who spent much time together were ridiculed. The supremacy of the collective, the ideology of pioneering comradeship, naturally saw families as divisive and threatening. The family is a potential centre of subversion, a focus of loyalty between the overarching collective and the individual, and could prevent the smooth functioning of the group.

But gradually things have changed with economic expansion and stabilisation. The early revolutionary ferment which fused the personal and collective ideals can only exist for a limited period, usually in an emergency. Out of it all the family is rising again. One article[16] has described how family housekeeping has come back – tea with the children at home, and even evening meals together apart, in the couple's own little flat. More personal equipment and a personal taste in decorations are emerging. Flexible clothing allowances are permitted so that distinctive clothing according to personal taste is possible. Women are reverting to a more expressive, home-centred role. There is a rising birth rate, and more parental oversight of the socialisation of children.

In the light of these two examples, it is difficult to resist the conclusion that whatever other arrangements are possible, the father + mother + child(ren) pattern of family life as we know it is a basic human obligation, and is indeed part of what C. S. Lewis called "the Tao" in *The Abolition of Man.*[17] Family life corresponds to the structure of practical reason, or the First Platitudes. Everywhere it is discovered to be the only way to achieve certain good ends and, indeed, to be somehow sensed as a good in itself.

## V

We turn finally to the "Western norm", which has been accepted by our civilisation for many centuries, and is sometimes thought of (rightly) as in addition the Christian norm. From possibilities, varieties and experiments, from the world of relativism, we come to a theologically validated pattern which Christians see as normative. In giving his views as to how the family should be organised, the Christian is not claiming greater insight – psychological, sociological, anthropological or any other. He is not saying that he sees better, understands better, how the family works. What he is saying is that as a steward of something handed down to him (that is, the revelation of Scripture) he has been entrusted with a blueprint, a "design" from the Maker of man and of families and of nations. This pattern tells him the best way for the micro-community – the family – to function.

At this point someone may object that this stance means simply descending into another strait-jacket of cultural relativism, that of the ancient Near East and the first century A.D. Roman Empire. This can be answered in two ways. We shall indeed be describing certain patterns which emerge from documents written in that area and in those periods. But the "choice" is far from arbitrary to the Christian mind. Firstly, the God of the Bible is a Sovereign God. Nothing happens by accident. He prepares nations, languages and cultural conditions so that in His time He speaks His Word with clarity and power, and men cannot mistake it. Paul wrote in Galatians 4: "When the time had fully come (or, as another translation puts it, "When the right time finally came") God sent forth His Son." It is that God, fully in charge of all events, who gave us this pattern and sealed particular social arrangements with divine approval in a very specific way.

The second answer would be that the God of the Bible can, if He wishes, speak a disruptive word to destroy, to change or to re-create. He can do so whenever it pleases Him. He is the Lord of complete innovation as well as of continuity and tradition, when He sees fit. If the paragraphs which follow strike the reader as "traditional" in any bad sense, then we may also need to bear in mind that the God who sanctified certain traditional patterns which men had come to see as beneficial can also innovate. He can produce a people without a King – a thing unheard of in the ancient world. He can produce a religion without an idol – a thing which the world had never seen when Israel began. He can produce a prophet without background, training or initiation. He can smash the age-long barrier between Jew and Gentile, and He can turn crucifixion into resurrection triumph. A God who can do that is not a God who can be confined in His world by any culturally relative patterns. His Word is never hampered or distorted or negated by cultural context. The Word of God can judge, and it can approve, items within the historical milieu into which it is spoken. Therefore, it can always be trusted.

We turn then to the teaching of the Bible. Firstly, the very words for "family" constitute an interesting study in themselves. Any Bible dictionary tells us that there are two words in the Old Testament and two in the New Testament, and they run roughly parallel – one from the Old being the equivalent of one from the New. The first pair consists of a Hebrew word meaning a circle of relatives or kinship group, often the extended kinship group. So that as well as "family" it can be translated "clan", "tribe" or "people". In the New Testament its partner seems to be a Greek word which is only used three times and whose root is the word for "father". It is used in Luke 2 : 4 (where Joseph is said to be "from the house and the family of David"), in Acts 3 : 25 (where Peter recalls the promise to Abraham that in his posterity all the families of the earth should be blessed) and – most significant – in Ephesians 3 : 15, to which we shall revert in a later chapter, where the Fatherhood of God is seen as the Archetype of all family relations. This is the relationship pair of words. It stresses paternity, kinship and descent.

The second pair consists of the usual Hebrew word for a house or dwelling in the Old Testament, and in the New Testament two closely related Greek words (*oikos* and *oikia*) whose primary meaning is also a building or a house. The transition from "house" to "home" or "family" is of course an obvious one. The essence here is the idea of place – physical togetherness. So we have the two pairs of words – one pointing to blood relationship and the other to locality.

In neither case have we a word exclusively for the nuclear family and that alone, unambiguously. The nuclear structure is indeed acknowledged as the centre of the house or the household. Two of the Ten Commandments are expressly concerned to preserve its integrity (Ex. 20 : 12 and

14). But it is rarely thought of as isolated. So perhaps the best word for "family" where it occurs in our Bible, might well be "household", rather than "family" in the restricted nuclear sense that we take it today.

When we examine the family structure as it takes shape in communities in the Old Testament, from the beginning up to Gensis 11 we discover an orderly pattern of family and clan relationships traced out in genealogies. Superficially this may seem to make for the great boredom of many of us as Bible-readers, with so many strange long names, but it is traced for a purpose. Lineage matters, and descent is important. Family and wider kinship patterns are assumed as giving continuity and identity. Even when we come to the Flood, God brings *families* into the ark. Then, with Abraham, something new happens. One man is called by grace, given promises, and becomes distinct as a family. That family is to become a nation. The family chronicles of Genesis 11–50 are packed to the very end of the book with intensely personal records of family life – jealousy and hatred, betrayal and revenge, scheming and deception, as well as forgiveness, faithfulness and joy. (Few can fail to sense the utter modernity of this ancient account, full of deep perceptions of the dynamics of family relations. It is no mere modern discovery that the family can be the focus of destructive urges, a place of damage and despair as well as of love and security. The Christian may recoil from the pessimism of Freud or Laing, but Scripture constantly warns about the way human sin can turn the potential for great blessing into the source of greatest damage and torment.)

The next stage is marked by the dramatic emergence of a tribe from Egypt at the time of the Exodus. Emergent Israel was a tribe which had gone down four hundred or more years previously as an extended family or clan under the patriarch Jacob. At their departure, they are gathered together in *families* to prepare for their deliverance, and they are provided with a lamb to be sacrificed for each *family*,

(Ex. 12 : 3). No sooner delivered from Egypt, their identity as the people of God is given structure. Their life is to be shaped by a code of moral standards, arrangements for law, arrangements for worship and for education – cultural transmission, by which the child shall know who he is and the group memory can be renewed. Notice that in the code which they are given, two of the basic Ten Commandments relate to the family – one to the vertical dimension (the child must honour his father and mother) and one to the horizontal (adultery is forbidden), preserving the sanctity of marriage (Ex. 20 : 12 & 14).

Further, arrangements have already been made for the renewal of the group memory in *families* by parental instruction. In each case the educational situation is a surprisingly modern one. It arises from the children's questions. "When you come to the land which the Lord will give you as He has promised, you shall keep this service. And when your children say to you 'What do you mean by this service?' you shall say . . ." (Ex. 12 : 26). John Dewey would have loved it! This is the experimental situation, the children's questioning leading to learning, advocated way back in the Old Testament.

Another provision is similar to the Passover memorial ceremony: "When in time to come your son asks you 'What does this mean?' you shall say to him 'By the strength of hand the Lord brought us out of Egypt from the house of bondage'" (Ex. 13 : 14). In that case it refers to the practice of dedicating the first-born males to God.

When we come to the New Testament, we recall that the first-century world commonly recognised the family unit as husband, wife, children, plus servants, dependant relatives and voluntary adherents who had joined the "household" by mutual consent – employees, friends and others.[18]

John the Baptist in so many ways links the Old and New Testaments; it is significant that we are given a detailed account of the preparation of his parents for his birth and ministry (as with several other great Old Testament leaders). The family has significance in the life and experience of the great deliverers whom God raises up (Moses, Samson, Gideon, Samuel, David, etc.) Jesus healed many at the request of relatives. The Gospel writers often note how tenderly he restored them to their families. On the cross He cared for Mary his mother so that she might be supported by an adopted "son" (John 19 : 26).

But there is also a dimension of challenge and pain for the disciple. The claims of Jesus were utterly uncompromising. Loyalty to Him must come first; the Kingdom of God took precedence over any human family. This is not surprising. God manifest in the flesh can and must demand our ultimate loyalty. In this context then we must face those hard sayings about hating the family and even hating one's own life (Luke 14 : 26). Family and possessions may have to be relinquished, Jesus stresses, "for My sake and the Gospel" (Mark 10 : 29). Jesus knew He had come to create the potential for conflict in many a family, setting one member against another. And He indicates that this conflict of loves would be itself a kind of crucifixion. It is significant that the bearing of the cross comes in Matthew 10 : 34–39, the very chapter where the hostility between mother, father and children is mentioned.

Yet this division is not the whole story. Once the primary allegiance to Jesus has been established, we need to remind ourselves of the other New Testament evidence. We must see clashing loyalties against the background of Our Lord's teaching that He came not to abolish but to fulfil. Jesus himself came into an earthly family and accepted the pattern of family living for thirty years, as Luke reminds us (surely with amazement) in Luke 2 : 51. His ministry brings healing and blessing to many a family. A hint at what is to come in the New Testament was given as early as Capernaum in the first months of Jesus' ministry, when he healed at a distance an official's son. The result was, we are told, that the father himself believed *and all his household* (John 4 : 53). John's

Gospel leaves us in no doubt that saving faith in the Son of God is an individual matter, yet here is a family response. And that is the regular pattern of New Testament evangelism. Once the Gospel is preached, family conversions and family baptisms are regular, e.g. Cornelius in Acts 10, Lydia and the jailor at Philippi in Acts 16. At Corinth we have Crispus (Acts 18 : 8) and also Stephanas (1 Corinthians 16 : 15) mentioned, both converted with their families.

The natural consequence of family conversions was family instruction in the faith. The Apostles' dual approach is significant. Their pattern was to teach in the temple *and at home* (Acts 5 : 42), or as Paul put it, "publicly and from house to house" (Acts 20 : 20). So family teaching in the home is practised as well as public teaching in the apostolic pattern of spreading the Gospel and building up the saints. Scholars have noticed how a "table" of basic family duties emerges, a list which is given three times at least (Col. 3, Eph. 5 and 1 Pet. 2). Surely this must be the outline of the regular apostolic instruction about family responsibilities. And instruction within the family goes on so that believing parents can be confident of having believing children. Noteworthy is the lovely example of Timothy with his mother and his grandmother, all believers (2 Tim. 1:5, 3:14–15, Titus 1: 5). Indeed, without a well-instructed and respectful family, a Christian man was not qualified for the office of overseer (1 Tim. 3 : 4) or of deacon (1 Tim. 3 : 12).

In summary, felt human need, the experience of the centuries and Scripture all speak in unison. Old and New Testaments are a continuity. Grace does not abolish nature – it perfects it. For all the radical newness of the Gospel, the New Testament simply restates God's plan for human living and growing at the most intimate level – the nuclear family. We emphasise however that it is not seen as a selfish or closed institution – it has open doors for others despite the uniqueness of the central complex of loyalties between husband, wife and children. The very words which are used in Scripture point towards the extended family ideal. Yet always the nuclear unit remains the fundamental structure, retaining its identity even within the new Israel, the Israel of God. The Kingdom of God indeed transcends the family – but the King gives us back the family renewed by His grace. It is not surprising therefore, to discover that Scripture lists sins against the family as sins both against revelation and against nature. The divinely given constitution, the very way we are made, demands this pattern and no other. Paul significantly lists disobedience to parents with the grossest of perversions in Romans 1, and with apocalyptic signs of the final dreadful moral declension of the last days in 2 Timothy 3 : 2.

There are many guidelines for the church today if we take this theology seriously. Evangelistic and pastoral work should take families into account more than they have done, rather than viewing the street, or the parish or even the city, or any other area, as simply a collection of atomised individuals to be "sown" or "reaped" or "edified". Again, the local church surely should act as an extended family, a context in which Christian families flourish and grow, a back-cloth – and also, from time to time, a safety net. Recent experiments in community living, some the result of the charismatic movement, some stemming from the "house church" ideal and others in more traditional settings, all point to a recognition of the need for regular wider human contact beyond the nuclear family, though containing it and feeding it at the same time. Ideally, such communities strengthen rather than weaken basic family ties. Is not the church called to reconstruct something akin to the older pre-industrial networks? Is not this the way to show love and appreciation for those without families – the widows and orphans repeatedly mentioned in Scripture, as well as the unmarried, the divorced, the illegitimate etc? Perhaps this is what the Spirit is calling the Church to see as an important factor in family renewal.

Then at the large community level, care for my neighbour

and a responsible social conscience will also mean care for the family in the national setting. A church vigilant for the family will work for its continuance, its stability, its enrichment and its rescue, both from introversion and a closed stagnation on the one hand (for the encastled family has concealed much poor parenting and damaging relationships in the past), and from easy dispersal and dissolution on the other.

It is of course possible so to stress the continuity of nature and grace, the apparent lack of innovation and fresh insight in the Christian picture which has been sketched above, that the objection might be made that there is no such thing as "the Christian family" there are only Christians living in different ages and countries, Christians *then* and *there*, culturally situated. The answer is to remind ourselves of the theological roots of all Christian thinking. In a somewhat individualistic article (whose extreme statements at some points this present author would not necessarily want to echo), the French Reformed scholar von Allmen wrote as follows:

> It is hardly likely that this biblical picture of the Christian family depends essentially on the social conditions of the ancient world, for it is too deeply rooted in the doctrine of the Fatherhood of God and the indissoluble unity that is between Christ and His Church. If social conditions change, then it will be the Church's task to discover in the new setting a form of family life where the core of the biblical teaching on the family can continue to flourish without alteration.[19]

Hence the Christian pastor or preacher can speak with complete assurance, not only to his own flock but to the whole society in which he lives. So on October 15th, 1975, Dr. Donald Coggan rightly set this truth at the heart of his Call to the Nation: "Give us strong, happy, disciplined families, and we shall be well on the way to a strong nation."[20]

CHAPTER TWO

# Marriage

Many variables in family patterns have been discerned by students of other civilisations and lands, as we have seen. Yet there is always a normative framework – everywhere we discover that the family is expected to be *this* rather than *that*, a network of kinship relationships which are discerned and obligations accepted. Everywhere mother, father and children lie at its heart, though responsibilities and wider links are almost always bound into an extended network, with various degrees of inclusion and extension to other persons outside the nuclear family. Attempts to do without the family as a basic and stabilising socialising agency, have been abandoned. The Biblical family unit (more correctly described as a "household", since both Old and New Testaments lack any word exclusively denoting the nuclear family) consists of parents, children plus grandparents and other relatives, servants and friends. The case for the family is thus established on the triple bases of communal experiment, social utility and a Christian understanding of man.

Now at the heart of every family stands a pair of persons, a man and a woman, and an institution which expresses and sanctions their unity – marriage. After underlining the importance of this topic, we shall survey the field from an anthropological or comparative point of view, then deal with the basis of marriage, particularly in today's society, and try to catch a glimpse of marriage "from the inside". Finally we shall again place this material in a Christian framework.

The importance of marriage can be discerned from at least four vantage points. Firstly, we note the way in which

every society has sought to regulate and provide a normative framework for the sexual relationships of adults. No
society has left its member complete freedom of action.
Secondly, structurally as a geometric pattern, marriage can
be seen as the very heart of family life. Psychologically too it
is central, for it initiates a new status – the shared life of two
partners – allowing the two to settle down before the arrival
of any children, and it thus becomes the basis and the background for the wider nuclear family as children come on to
the scene and grow up, and the source of their stability.
Every society recognises the need to structure the way
human beings come together and grants some form of ritual
recognition to this situation. Thirdly, as we know from our
own difficult and disturbed epoch, the breakup of marriage
causes immense personal distress and damage, which
resonates out into the social sphere. The health of marriage
is obviously of crucial importance for social well-being. And
fourthly, the positive "use" of marriage can prove such an
enrichment and a blessing, especially since we live in an
increasingly mechanised and impersonal society where relationships are more casual and discontinuous, and where
other psychological bonds have become weaker. For this,
marriage to a very large degree can compensate.

## I

We turn now to consider the patterns of marriage as a social
institution. Marriage at its shortest definition is the
socially-recognised econonomic and sexual relationship
between one or more men and one or more women. It is,
empirically, a pattern regulated by social custom. Marriage
is a state which involves specific tasks seen as rights and
obligations. We often tend to think of marriage as only, or
principally, concerned with sexual access. But it has also
always involved interdependence and economic co-operation, and in this way it unites the economic and the sexual. It
is for this reason characterised by co-habitation. Hence the
emergence of "home" – both a *place* and a *relationship* in

which the next generation is protected and socialised. The essential dimensions of the married state are therefore protection, home-making, economic support, sexual access and responsibility for children. As these tasks are ascribed in the patterns of marriage in various societies they form a settled framework of expectations for the individuals in those societies as they contemplate marriage, and embark upon it. George Murdock, an American sociologist, in his book *Social Structures*[1] took account of two hundred and fifty societies and found that the nuclear family was universal and the basic social grouping. The family, he found, is characterised by common residence (the home), economic co-operation and reproduction, this last implying "a socially approved sexual relationship". It is a fact, as we shall see, that societies restrict sexual privilege. But never, comments Murdock, between married partners. Thus a powerful instinctual drive is canalised in a predictable and socially useful way. The sex drive thus reinforces reciprocal and co-operative habits which characterise the family unit in the other dimensions of its social existence.

However, not every community restricts sexual intercourse exclusively to married persons. This is an excusable but incorrect deduction from *our* use of the term "marriage", in the western Christian sense. In Murdock's two hundred and fifty societies, sixty-five allowed the unmarried, unrelated adults to have unrestricted sexual access to members of the other sex, and twenty others gave qualified consent to premarital promiscuity. Only fifty-four disapproved of premarital liaisons between non-relatives. And in a significant number a married male could legitimately engage in an extra-marital sexual relationship with a female relative.

In a count of over four hundred societies, Hobhouse, Wheeler and Ginsberg[2] found only sixty-six showed the monogamous pattern. Three hundred and seventy-eight sanctioned polygyny (that is more than one wife per man), and thirty-one polyandry (that is, more than one husband for one woman). Of course this rather crude count takes no account of the size, durability, character or quality of the societies themselves, but the figures show the variety of permitted marriage patterns – as well as pointing to a degree of male dominance and potential exploitation through polygamy in the majority which today would seem unacceptable.

We cannot omit to mention the fascination – at least for the anthropologists – of the incest taboo. Certain close relationships – *always* those within the nuclear family, and with varying additional near relatives in different societies – are forbidden any expression of sexual intimacy. To quote the distinguished sociologist Talcott Parsons, "the incest taboo is a universal of human societies."[3] Anthropologists and sociologists now see this as an essential link between sex and society. The family makes society possible by prescribing, usually in some sort of rule of exogamy (that is, the convention of only marrying outside your primary family group) a wider patterned social exchange of sexual partners. The husband or wife must come from outside the immediate household, the family in which the individual's closest blood relatives live and where the growing child obtains his primary orientation. That particular field is forbidden for the choice of spouse. It is this constant interchange of mates between families which ensures a wider cultural and community integration; a feeling of social "belonging" and continuity which makes a society. The alternative would be for the closest emotional ties (that is those within the nuclear family itself) to be expressed sexually, with the result that the ties between some individuals might perhaps be deepened, but such bonds only exist between fewer and fewer individuals, and cease to reinforce the wider society itself. Families would thus become introverted, and atomisation of emotional involvement would weaken the whole social fabric. Modern genetic studies of the harmful results of in-breeding only reinforce our awareness of the dangers. The warnings of Sigmund and Sieglinde, of Oedipus and Jocasta still stand.

On the positive side, the incest taboo makes an important dimension of social exchange more likely. Families become linked by giving and receiving their young adults in marriage. A solidarity transcending that of the nuclear family is established; eroticism is regulated and the individual is propelled (Talcott Parsons' own word) out of the nuclear family into the wider society. There he or she assumes both non-familial roles which society always needs, and most often founds his or her own new nuclear family by marriage.[4]

I turn now to the various types of marriage pattern in different societies and ask what advantages scholars have perceived in the different types of sexual regulation. One of the most significant studies here has been that of J. D. Unwin, whose book *Sex and Culture* is undoubtedly one of the monumental works of comparative anthropology. Written in 1932 and published by the Oxford University Press two years later, this book of six hundred and seventy-five pages is a leisurely, detailed and exhaustive account of an inquiry. Unwin describes his investigation as follows:

> When I started these researches I sought to establish nothing, and had no idea of what the result would be. With care-free open-mindedness I decided to test, by a reference to human records, a somewhat startling conjecture that had been made by the analytical psychologists. This suggestion was that if the social regulations forbid direct satisfaction of the sexual impulses the emotional conflict is expressed in another way, and that what we call "civilisation" has always been built up by compulsory sacrifices in the gratification of innate desires.[5]

Unwin selected only societies for which sufficient evidence could be found (a) of sexual regulation and (b) of what he calls "cultural energy". This latter he defined as a process perceived as tending towards refinement, elegance, exactitude, a drive towards questioning, exploring and conquering. His studies covered eighty primitive societies[6] and sixteen civilised societies[7] and his two general conclusions were as follows:

1. The cultural condition of any society in any geographical environment is conditioned by its past and present methods of regulating the relations between the sexes.[8]

2. No society can display productive social energy unless a new generation inherits a social system under which sexual opportunity is reduced to a minimum.[9]

The Western Christian norm received startling support from this research. *The greatest energy*, Unwin comments, *has been displayed only by those societies which have reduced their sexual opportunity to a minimum by the adoption of absolute monogamy.*[10]

Thus Unwin confirmed, by meticulous and thoughtful amassing of a vast amount of evidence, that the gloomy observations of Freud, though founded on what may appear a jaundiced view of human nature, did correspond to empirical data on the macro-sociological level. Freud believed that only by communal renunciation of instinctual gratification could civilisation arise and a society continue to exist. He believed that culture springs from the denial of instincts. Art, science and technology arise from the restraint of aggression, sex and avarice. Unwin showed results which were consistent with this theory, though he professed ignorance of the "why" and even the "how". He concluded that the evidence pointed towards a choice: either cultural energy and achievement, or sexual licence. It is impossible for any society to enjoy *both* for more than one generation. Aldous Huxley examined Unwin's evidence in his book *Ends and Means* (1965), as did Dr. David Mace,[11] and both found his evidence compelling. The way in which Unwin's work has been almost completely ignored by both scholars and popular writers sometimes seems positively sinister.

In looking back on this evidence briefly sketched above it is worth observing that for centuries societies have seemed to know that they *should* regulate sexual conduct and the formation of families in some way. It is only in the twentieth century that we are seeing the advantages of this in the light of sociological, anthropological and psychological enquiry. Doubtless there has always been a basic awareness that with roughly fifty per cent of each sex being born, when young adults wish to establish their own families, it will prevent endless strife if individuals make up their minds about a mate and then have to stick to their decision! Doubtless too, men and women have always been aware that children need a particular pair to care for them – to protect and to induct them into the society's culture. Nevertheless, there seems to be a deep awareness of something beyond these consider- ations of mere communal prudence. The event of choosing an adult mate is both joyful and solemn, significant for the individuals concerned and for the community. Rules and ritual point to its importance. There are prohibited kinship degrees and there are limitations on the future behaviour of the partners concerned. And there are particular patterns of limitation which seem to benefit society more than others. For the good of the family itself and for the welfare of society, marriage must be firmly rooted in communal aware- ness, in the network of roles and institutions, of law and convention; it must continue as a topic of study and celebra- tion, of drama and debate. From the earliest societies onwards the message seems to be: we neglect marriage at our peril.

It is sometimes argued by today's favourite media advisers that it is far better for young people not to enter any long-term commitment (i.e. marriage) until they have found out whether they can live happily together, including sexual experiment. But there are many considerations which suggest that this is not the way forward to a productive relationship for the two people concerned, and certainly not in the interests of the wider society. It is an un- stable middle state, neither married nor single. The com- munity is uncertain how to treat such couples. Nor will they know themselves just where they are. They will be uncertain of each other. They will continue in ignorance as to what it would *really* be like to be married, because no-one is ever able to experience what it means to be married until an exclusive, total, public commitment to one other person has been made. No amount of sexual experiment beforehand will tell you what being married is going to be like. Of course young people should get to know each other. There are many pointers towards suitability through going out together, compatibility of interests, advice of friends, a period of engagement, etc. But sexual union symbolises and seals the deepest commitment of all, and should be kept for marriage. There is a further difficulty with sexual experiment. After so-called "trial marriage" has begun, when should it end? How does one know the trial has failed? As for sexual compatibility – might there not be someone else with whom it could be even better? The theory traps the young person in the logic (if not always the practice) of an unending series of experiments. Even if each new girl is better than the last one – how does the serious young male experimenter tell when he has reached the point of saying "Yes, this is the one?" Many societies have conceded some premarital experiment, as we have noted. But the Christian view is saner, and a practicable one to commend to young people.

## II

But what are the bases on which marriages are established? "How do I find a life partner?" is a justified question from a partly socialised youngster in any culture. He is right to expect guidance from his elders. It is significant to discover that the question "What were you looking for when you agreed to marry?" is the crucial probe of the modern therapist as he or she seeks to unravel a marital tangle. Such questions have been answered very differently by different societies at different times. In the past, marriages have been commonly arranged by parents. Dynastic unions between royal families, amongst the nobility and later within the new aristocracy of industrial ownership – all are well known features of our own history.

Parental decisions had to be carried out. But the practice has been far more widespread, as we find when we examine the literature. In traditional rural China, marriages were arranged by family elders even among the poorest peasants.[12] Respect for elders and a patriarchal pattern of family life obviously support this practice, but it may be immensely strengthened by political considerations amongst tribal chiefs, the crowned heads of nations and by similar factors of power, wealth, prestige and inheritance in the upper strata of many types of society.

By contrast with this, contemporary Western practice is the free choice of both partners on the basis of mutual attraction – what one American sociologist has called "non-expedient personal preference".[13]

For at least two centuries European literature and sensibility has presented us with what is still the most popular concept of the ideal – what is often referred to as "romantic love". Yet there is here a source of much confusion, since it contains two elements which (though both verbally expressed as "love") can exist independently of each other – intense physical attraction (with a strong sexual element) on the one hand, and what C. S. Lewis calls "delighted pre-occupation" with someone "admirable in herself"[14] on the other. The importance of this distinction is crucial. There are two elements not one. The coming of Freudian reductionism to the debate in our cultural market place suggests there is *really* only one thing – sex. Over-simplifications of this kind have wrought havoc with many of our ideals and finer feelings, and even with necessary logical distinctions in our discussion of human motivation and human behaviour.

Lewis in his book *The Four Loves* helps us to see the distinction quite starkly. *Venus* is his name for carnal sexual desire. It is common to us and to the beasts (though they vary seasonally in a way which human beings do not) and it aims at sensory pleasure. It contains no element of the personal or individual; Venus seeks experience, gratifi-

cation, sensory pleasure. This is simply a fact about ourselves. *Eros* on the contrary is about the beloved as a unique
person; it discovers his or her individual qualities and an
intense appreciation of their worth and splendour. Eros
does not aim at happiness – Eros can demand allegiance
without happiness, sacrifice without satisfaction. Here is
how Lewis sums it up:

> Sexual desire without Eros, wants *it*, the *thing in itself*; Eros wants
> the Beloved.
>    The *thing* is a sensory pleasure; that is, an event occurring within
> one's own body. We use a most unfortunate idiom when we say, of a
> lustful man prowling the streets, that he "wants a woman". Strictly
> speaking, a woman is just what he does not want. He wants a
> pleasure for which a woman happens to be the necessary piece of
> apparatus. How much he cares about the woman as such may be
> gauged by his attitude to her five minutes after fruition (one does not
> keep the carton after one has smoked the cigarettes). Now Eros
> makes a man really want, not a woman, but one particular woman.
> In some mysterious but quite indisputable fashion the lover desires
> the Beloved herself; not the pleasure she can give.[15]

Our problem today is that we do not know how to relate
these two meanings or components in setting standards for
the marriages of tomorrow. Venus has never had it so good.
The pornographic magazine has been supplemented by the
pornographic film and the pornographic theatre. There is
ample fuel for male lust. In print, picture and on the stage
masturbation, copulation and sexual conjunction both
natural and unnatural is set before us. And it certainly sells.
Of this fiery but transient stimulus we are accustomed to use
the words "make love". Like so many powerful errors, the
verbal expression and its link with marriage has an element
of truth, which we might list in the following propositions:

   1) husbands ought to love their wives, wives ought to love
their husbands, and this love can be expressed in sexual con-
juction. (This is a commonplace of the wisdom of the elders
in every culture.)

   2) marriage is ordained to regulate the expression and
enjoyment of sexual desire. (This is a common feature in all
known societies).

3) many marriages began with little between the partners but sexual desire. As Lewis wrote in the same work:

> Most of our ancestors were married off in early youth to partners chosen by their parents on grounds that had nothing to do with Eros.
> They went to the act with no other "fuel", so to speak, than plain animal desire. And they did right; honest Christian husbands and wives, obeying their fathers and mothers, discharging to one another their "marriage debt", and bringing up families in the fear of the Lord. [16]

Yet mere Venus is no adequate basis for *choosing* a partner, since Venus provides no indication of any substantial degree of compatability between the partners over time, nor of the potential for mutual helpfulness and support. In past ages parental influence provided some objective check of suitability in a wider social setting. Even today like tends to marry like with respect to class, race, religion, age, intelligence and education level, according to the sociologists. But in today's fluid and mobile society, with its suspicion of all distinctions, whether acquired or inherited, these things matter less. And it can scarcely be denied that a marriage founded on Venus alone has an insecure basis. As the sociologist Ernest van den Haag writes:

> The sexual act itself may serve as a vehicle for numberless feelings: lust, vanity and self-assertion, doubt and curiosity, possessiveness, anxiety, hostility, anger or indifferent release from boredom. [17]

Of course, Eros – a delighted estimate of the worth of one's marriage partner – can in principle come later. Doubtless it did in many of the arranged marriages of the past. But since society still invests so much of its future in the setting up of a household which will provide the citizens of the future, surely we need to encourage a culture in which Venus is restrained, while Eros is honoured as the one necessary component in "being in love".

Yet again we need to enter a caveat. Marriages can succeed without the admiring preoccupation of Eros. Indeed as Lewis points out, Eros himself can on occasion break marriages, assume a god-like domain over the individual and become demonic. The Triston story retains its warnings as well as its attractive power for this very reason. It broke the marriage of King Mark. Yet if Eros is to be rightly placed and a continual delight, and if Venus is to be properly enjoyed and satisfied, the consensus of social wisdom seems to point to marriage. There, and there only, is the right context for such exchanges. Might we not agree in purely secular terms therefore, that our young people should be encouraged to distinguish between Eros and Venus? that awakening Eros between two persons is the best basis for marriage in today's open society? that when Venus comes first she is likely to blind and confuse? that it is Eros which dignifies Venus? and that neither Eros nor Venus can justify a man or a woman intruding into the marriage relationship of two persons who have already vowed themselves to each other and publicly promised to remain together and thereby to found a family? These are questions which common prudence and social responsibility demand that we answer affirmatively.

We shall be strengthened in this resolve if we recall that though marriage is an intensely personal relationship, if we are forced to give any priority, we must say that marriage exists for the family, rather than vice versa. It is a social institution, establishing in the eyes of society a new nuclear unit, involving an exchange of solemn and binding vows in public, a change of name and an assumption of new legal and moral responsibilities. Indeed, one view of marriage goes so far as to see all social arrangements in connection with marriage as a complex ritual with one aim – preventing the anti-social and unproductive involvement of husband and wife in a dyadic relationship which could tempt the partners to become unconscious of all other social obligations. Dyadic withdrawal (that is, the tendency of two people to be completely bound up with each other and unaware of anyone else) to the psychiatrist Philip Slater[18] threatens to short-circuit the community network and drain off its source of sustenance. He therefore describes the marriage ceremony as the community's own "intrusion ritual" into the close and deepening emotional relationship of the two partners as the marriage approaches. The two families get involved; the church or the legal officers have to be informed and prepared. Financial and housing matters come to the fore. The wedding hospitality has to be planned, with its lists of guests and presents and so on. The the couple come to feel at last in desperation that they are only playing a minor role, that they are relatively passive; Slater believes that at this stage the whole idea of elopement arises in many cases! But he suggests that the couple say to each other at this point, "It's already gone too far now, and we shall have to go through with it." It is not necessary to accept Slater's case *in toto* to see that there is a social importance in marriage which is unconsciously stressed by our community in this whole pattern of arrangements.

We have now seen how the basis of marriage contains elements and emphases from three sources – the sexual, the personal and the social. The needs of the individual for physical satisfaction, for personal delight in another and for social significance are paralleled by society's need to regulate sexual behaviour, to delineate kinship patterns and obligations, to maintain social stability and to ensure the socialisation of the young.

## III

The internal dynamics of marriage are infinitely varied. Evidently they will differ according to the more obvious variables – number of spouses (monogamy/polygamy), number of progeny, wider kinship affiliation, age and economic status of spouses, together with the particular social background, the ideological, historical and geographical factors which give the surrounding culture its particular economic and political character, and hence its role pattern for married persons. But there is not space to spread the net any wider than our own Western European post-industrial society.

What happens within marriage in our society today? Or to put it more precisely, what are the expectations with which individuals enter marriage? Let us begin by noting that marriage as it has always been understood involves role differentiation. Husband and wife undertook, and were expected to undertake, different tasks. As long as these time-honoured distinctions continued to be transmitted and accepted unquestioningly – perhaps unconsciously – at least married partners knew what they were aiming at.

Marital role definition has its roots in the basic physical differences between male and female. The physical differences between the sexes which constitute their different reproductive functions are genetically determined, irreversible and universal. These biological variations are used by most societies as a basis for the designation of behaviour, attitudes and personality factors considered appropriate to each sex. But the differences exist apart from any cultural patterns, at least in the following respects: at birth the average girl is smaller and lighter than the average boy, but is physically more developed; a maturational lead of between four – six weeks has been posited. By the age of seventeen years the average boy is some eighty per cent physically stronger than the average girl, though the male is more vulnerable to disease, defects and the influence of an unfavourable environment than the female. Even in the first three weeks of life, more than twice as many males die from infection, and this differential in resistance to disease continues throughout life. There are differences in behaviour and mood due to the physical changes of the menstrual cycle. However, the most obvious physical differences are of those concerned with the reproductive process and it is the reproductive function and all its social implications which constitute the most significant difference between the sexes.

On the basis of these physical differences the stereotypes of male and female attitudes have been erected, desirable qualities and specific contributions to society, to the family and to marriage. Broadly speaking the tradition has been for the man to be occupationally orientated, performing tasks outside the home, relating and representing the family to the wider society, offering protection and determining status. His is an *instrumental* function, requiring leadership, decision and authority. The wife and mother on the other hand performs an *expressive* function, providing emotional support and comfort to the family; she offers warmth, gentleness, affection, caring support and the indefinable "tone" of the family home.

It is a matter of dispute as to how far the known personality and attitude differences between men and women are to be attributed to innate biological factors, and how far they are the consequence of socially acquired stereotypes which pattern the development of the whole personality from the moment the sex of the child is discovered at birth. We shall indicate those psychological differences which do exist, remembering that they are only statistical tendencies or averages (i.e. what we discover empirically to be the case when surveys are made) and on each side they represent a tendency to polarity rather than clear-cut categories. In other words, a few women will be found to have strongly marked characteristics classified well over into what we normally would think of as the male category, and some (though not many) men will be found to possess attributes which situate them well over towards the female end of the spectrum.

Cognitive differences are well documented by many researchers, and it has been found that females perform better on verbal tests, arithmetical tasks, clerical skills, some kinds of verbal reasoning, rote memory and fine manual dexterity. On the other hand men do better on spatial tasks, mechanical and practical tasks and mathematical problem-solving. We need to recall however that psychological test performance registers more than pure innate ability. Emotional maturity, motivation, self-concepts, social pressures and so on are also involved.

Turning to non-cognitive differences, we find that in the

field of personality testing (mainly in Europe and America) certain well-known dimensions show significant statistical differences between the two sexes. On the whole these surveys show that women tend to be tender-minded, dependent and sensitive, whereas men tend to be tough-minded, self-reliant and realistic. Men are inclined to be assertive, independent, aggressive, competitive and stubborn, while women are drawn towards a model which is humble, mild, accommodating and conforming. From this emerge the sex stereotypes, so much deplored by the women's liberation movements.

How do these findings relate to marriage? There can be no doubt that marital expectations and conjugal behaviour have been – and probably will increasingly be – affected by the current controversies over the social stereotype of woman and wife. There is no longer complete agreement on this polarity – instrumental/expressive, tough-minded/tender-minded and so on. Some women have always found it difficult to adjust to such a role. If they happened also to be gifted, single and of high social status, like Elizabeth I or Florence Nightingale, they could be tolerated and even admired. But only in our own decade has there been a strident wholesale rejection of the female role in its traditional sense. Women's "liberation" thinking sees the above pattern as an enslaving social artefact and a non-material chain from which women must be freed.

There is today less controversy than there once was about the single woman in the world of work, where occupational opportunity is now in principle open to all, irrespective of sex. But if the expressive stereotype is rejected wholesale, two things will result. Firstly, the cultivation of the very characteristics which made, for example, a good nurse, will no longer be socially signalled as especially desirable in half the population (i.e. women) and the danger is that though they will be in theory held out as desirable ideals for *any* person irrespective of sex, they will in fact be sought after by no-one; especially if the pay is poor.

Secondly, abolition of the stereotypes has important results in marriage, in particular. Neither partner will be certain what his or her *specific* contribution to the home should be. Some matters have been traditionally left to the male and are now rightly shared. In illness or bereavement it has long been acknowledged that the wife may need to be a bread-winner or the husband a homemaker. But now the two-income households offer not only increasing affluence to many marriages (though disappointment and frustration where health or other reasons forbid it) but also a welcome widening of the mental and social horizons to many wives. Furthermore, this new flexibility in marriage roles prevents the bitter sneer at traditional marriages that they represent a crude impersonal transaction, where the woman comes to trade sexual favours in return for being economically supported – a "sexual bargaining system" as one sociologist calls it. While possibly appealing to market economists, the lovelessness of this pattern is repellent, and we cannot deny that in past generations it was a reality. In mitigation however it might be answered that even this formulation of marriage (at its inception), does leave room for love to grow within the framwork of a monogamous commitment, if sincerely promised and seriously intended, even though tenderness and understanding may not be present at the beginning.

The stereotype had its uses. It prevented severe identity crises, provided models, channelled affection, directed instincts, protected certain sensitive areas from harmful experiment and hence avoided friction. It also, alas, institutionalised a species of male dominance which could deny basic liberties and possibilities of personal growth and social usefulness to women. So with these gains and losses, where are we today?

In examining marital roles, any community needs first to make up its mind about a number of quite clear-cut issues: What is marriage? What do we want it to be and to mean? Is this to be seen as a permanent commitment? Is this an exclusive commitment? Is this a totally symmetrical relationship or should there be some social recognition of asymmetry? How shall we stigmatise departure from the norm? How important are children? What is marriage intended to provide? How do we characterise and allow for breakdown? There must be social agreement if the expectations of the next generation are to be given any coherent shape. But what criteria shall we use? These questions are with us today in an acute form, and our society is deeply confused. It is to this confusion that these pages are addressed, and that the Christian Church has so much to offer.

Let us start at a less abstract and more practical level. Given a modern marriage, what can be made of it? There are positive things to say. Broadly speaking, modern thoughtful investigation draws attention to the closeness, the subtlety and the great potential richness of the inner working of the marriage relationship today. Conditions in many ways favour this. Survival is no longer a pressing and urgent daily issue; life lasts longer; people marry at a younger age; affluence and automation increase available time and social options in work and leisure. We may indicate some features of our new and deeper understanding of the relationship in marriage under two headings: cognitive and affective, i.e. referring first to the intellectual and then to the emotional aspects.

On the cognitive level it is increasingly recognised that marriage is a shared enterprise in the construction of a new framework of reality. In a celebrated article Peter Berger and Hansfried Kellner[19] point out that every society has its own way of defining and perceiving reality: what makes sense and how experience is to be interpreted. For social coherence and communal intelligibility these shared meanings need constant clarification and re-statement. The same holds good for the individual as he perceives and defines *his* world, and crucially, his identity and his place within it. This constant validation, which is a human need, comes through the actions of significant others, especially through their speech. As these writers put it:

> The plausibility and stability of the word as socially defined is dependent upon the strength and certainty of significant relationships in which conversation about this world can continually be carried on.[20]

Having recognised that fact, it is obvious that marriage will have a special position among these validating relationships.

These two authors point out that marriage is "a dramatic act in which two strangers come together and re-define themselves". They do not have a shared past, but from now on their daily face-to-face contact means that for each of them there is a new centre of significant conversation – and a constant correlation and readjustment of definitions and horizons. The world is being reconstructed – in bed and over the breakfast table. The result is "a hardening or stabilisation of the common objectivated reality". This includes the married couple's images of other people, self-definitions and even a reconstruction of the world of past reality. Typically this process is unapprehended. But the fact that it does take place means that we must see marriage not simply as stepping into new roles, but stepping into a new world.

This description (and a brief summary is quite inadequate to convey the subtlety and the many fruitful insights of the analysis in the article itself) allows us to glimpse two factors. Firstly, there is the need for conversation – for constant interchange of ideals, fears, hopes, doubts and longings, together with views of people and events, past and present. Much family therapy today is aimed simply at restoring communication which has been interrupted; usually as a result of some blockage, the partners are in a very real sense, living in two different worlds.

Secondly, this analysis points to the need for generally shared definitions and expectations of the marriage relationship itself. Without this, marital adjustment may well be impossible, or almost unbearably painful. At present, with

Berger and Kellner, we can still be confident of the greater stability of married, as against unmarried, individuals. The two writers point out that this has been established by many surveys, and the reason they point to is simply that "the married individual comes to live in a more stable world", since each partner is constantly validating and strengthening the other partner's view – through conversation and interchange – of the world outside.

But an increase in pluralism and in mutually exclusive meanings and universes of discourse within a society might well bring us to the point where marriage for many individuals might be an impossible task, due to cognitive dissonance between all the partners available. Pluralism of values, ideals, stereotypes, roles and expectations is a recipe for the dissolution of a society. Conflict and discord in social aspirations may make good TV drama but it will not make good citizens. A community can only fly apart if its members cease to share a common moral vision and a consequent network of ideals for roles and institutions. Whatever democracy may mean, it must not be allowed to suggest *this* kind of pluralism. The significance of the mass media in this context is of the utmost importance. *Cross-Roads* and *Coronation Street* can do more for marriage – for good or ill – than most Christians have yet recognised.

From the cognitive we turn to the affective side. In his rich and illuminating writings on marriage, Dr. Jack Dominian, the distinguished London psychiatrist, stresses that marriage is above all a focus of sustenance, healing and growth.[21] *Sustenance* is the willingness to care and support, to protect and cherish. Despite increasing sexual equality, husband and wife will probably never care and support each other in quite the same way. There is always a two-way interchange but attitudes are not identical; this can only be a cause for rejoicing. Yet mutual interdependence is more complex than the simpler formulation of exclusive sex roles, based on one hundred per cent dominance on one side and one hundred per cent submission on the other. Diversity without stifling dominance is more human and in the end more fruitful.

*Healing* acknowledges that each of us has reached adulthood to some degree marred, distorted or hurt by parents, by so-called friends and even by "the way life has treated us". The closeness of modern marriage and its open, frank quality are the ideal conditions for the spontaneous expression of frustration, anger, guilt and resentment resulting from these earlier experiences. A sharing of feelings can take place, with the provision of trust, affection, acceptance or approval, which may well have been missing at an earlier stage. Above all, the sense of inadequacy or un-worthiness can be wonderfully healed by the experience of being loved and valued just for one's own unique self-hood. This is the very opposite of valuing someone for their "performance" – for what they do, or get, or achieve.

*Growth* involves the maturing of the two individuals and in particular the discovery of their potential – the potential of one's marriage partner. Trust and understanding are needed so that (as with a growing child) the security of a reliable and predictable partner provides the encourage-ment of a significant other who is "always there". On this basis gifts and talents can be revealed, tested without fear and fostered into a wider usefulness which will bring personal satisfaction as well as social benefit.

It scarcely needs saying that insecurity will play havoc with the potential of marriage in these respects. The con-tinuity guaranteed by a solemn covenant to exclusive life-long fidelity is the needed guarantee of this security, and the basis on which these enriching exchanges of affection, affirmations of value (and hence healing) and nurture can take place.

There can be no doubt that despite our deeper understanding of human communication, of individual emotional needs, of joint cognitive enterprises in "world-building" and of the unique potential enrichment of the marriage relationship, marriage itself is less stable today. Divorce has been made easier in Britain, and every year more couples take steps to "end" their marriage in this way. Christian people, who are not exempted from the rigours of our climate or the dangers of disease or road accident, find themselves also (with their fellow-citizens) increasingly liable to the hazards of marital breakdown. Part of the problem is certainly caused by heightened expectations of individuals marrying, especially in the realm of sexual satisfaction – the pornographic magazines aimed at men and the constant discussion of female orgasm in women's journals have contributed largely to this climate. Then again, the cult of instant pleasure which has shaped every aspect of the youth culture since the 1960s makes it much harder to undertake a task whose rewards come mostly in the longer term. Marriage has always needed "working at", many months of basic adjustment to a new shared life-style being followed by years of less discernible (but equally important) self-denial and restraint, with an occasional landmark of deliberate self-sacrifice. The delights and joys are there, but they do not all come at once, and often they come unbidden. The patient and deliberate dedication to the happiness and well-being of another person is what Christians mean by "love". Self-denying love demands the continuing application to the task of "making a marriage work". Many of today's young married folk have such a poor grasp of this fundamental demand – the one thing needful. Their grandparents knew what it meant. Frequently married couples seem dazed by the challenge of *strain* – when one partner develops a serious illness, faces long-term unemployment, advances socially or intellectually or professionally and appears to "leave behind" the other partner, etc. Yet the promises were clear – "for richer for poorer, in sickness and in health . . . till death".

## IV

So we turn quite naturally to the Christian framework in which these facts must be situated. As with so many other human problems, we find that the framework is already there in human experience, apprehended more clearly in some ages than in others, and yet dimly perceived by man even without the clear-cut revelation of Holy Scripture. Again, therefore, Christians find in the Bible a pattern standing out clearly, towards which (the social scientists show us) societies ancient and modern have been cautiously groping. Let us briefly review the Biblical pattern, which fits the facts like a glove to the hand.

In Genesis 1 : 27–28 we read that God made man male and female. There in that first chapter He put man and wife on equal parity and commanded them jointly to rule the earth and to produce children. A deeper complementarity is hinted at in Genesis 2 : 18–25 where the narrative speaks symbolically of the making of Eve out of Adam, and we have the phrase used which is taken up in the New Testament referring to marriage, "one flesh". Genesis 2 : 24 in particular is quoted by our Lord in Matthew 19:4–6 where He speaks of the absolute primacy and centrality of the new relationship formed in marriage. It is when a man leaves his family of origin, in particular his father and mother, that he comes to "cleave to his wife" and a fresh unit emerges. And this is a new primary loyalty, a new basic allegiance which over-rides other allegiances. In the New Testament we find that our Lord himself had an earthly home, significantly, despite his virgin birth; that Mary and Joseph in fact married; that Jesus graced a wedding for his first miracle (John 2) and that the New Testament writers therefore refer to marriage as an excellent and holy thing (Heb. 13 : 4) and point out that to forbid marriage is in fact a devilish error which must not be found in the Church (1 Tim. 4 : 1–5). At the same time, and realistically, marriage is seen to be in some aspects a remedy for the disorder caused by sin (1 Cor. 7 : 1–8).

But there is an even deeper dimension to which we have been introduced by the thought of Jesus himself as the Bridegroom. He spoke of Himself in these terms as early as

Mark 2 : 20. This is expanded in the wonderful passage in Ephesians 5, where the relationship between Christ and His people, those whom He has come to save, is viewed as analogous to the marriage relationship. Headship and sacrifice are the two themes which are sounded in that particular chapter. This whole pattern is glorified in the very last chapters of the New Testament (Rev. 21 & 22), where the Church is seen as the Bride of Christ and the spiritual union is consummated.

This rich and positive approach to marriage must not blind us to the fact that the Bible speaks of the single life as a calling. Celibacy can be a gift from God (Jer. 16, Matt. 19 : 10–12, 1 Cor. 7:7). Our Lord Himself was perfect, yet unmarried. In the early Church a particular ministry for the unmarried was recognised; the Apostle Paul himself was unmarried. But Scripture balances this by a pattern of hospitality and care which the homes of married people provide for the unmarried, the widows and others.

Biblical realism and the picture of man as sinful by nature means that there are negative statements too concerning the breaking of the marriage pattern. Certain things are clearly forbidden. Bigamy, polygamy and concubinage are found in the Old Testament, and even found among the people of God, but on every occasion they spell disaster. They are never there with God's express blessing and approval. They are a pathetic second best. Adultery is solemnly forbidden, and is listed as one of those sins deserving the death penalty (Lev. 20 : 10); fornication, extra-marital sex or pre-marital sexual activity is often linked in Scripture with prostitution, and unfaithfulness of other kinds like idolatry (e.g. Rev. 22 : 15). The warnings of Proverbs (e.g. chapters 5 and 7) against sexual laxity (prostitution) are remarkable, while in the New Testament, these are things which define a life-style alienated from God (e.g. Eph. 4 : 17–24). Sexual perversions (e.g. bestiality, homosexual practices) are listed as abominations in both Old and New Testaments; they are unthinkable for Christians as contrary to the Gospel (1 Tim.

1 : 10) and to creation order (Rom. 1 : 18–27), and exclude a man from God's kingdom (1 Cor. 6 : 9).[22] Likewise incest (1 Cor. 5 : 1–2). These latter practices also attracted the death penalty in Israel (Lev. 20 : 11–16).[23].

Death frees a surviving marriage partner from all previous marital obligations (Rom. 7 : 1–2). And a marriage itself can, it seems, be terminated by the deliberate destructive behaviour of one or both partners while both are still alive. So there are provisions in Scripture, sadly, for divorce (Matt. 5 : 32, 19 : 9, 1 Cor. 7 : 10–16). Whether the Church can ever celebrate a second marriage with a good conscience when one (or both) of the covenanting parties has a partner still living, to whom identical vows were made, is an agonising problem. Perhaps in the nature of the case no general rule can be given, neither a total negative, nor an easy acceptance, nor a formula to distinguish case from case.

In the light therefore of this very brief survey of the Scriptural data we have witnessed a positive pattern emerging – and not only from the Bible, but from the facts of human experience. From the same two sources we are warned that pre-marital sexual experiment, adultery, prostitution and perversion are hostile both to trusting and productive relationships on a personal level and to social coherence and cultural enrichment. Sexual permissiveness undermines not only marriage but society itself. Is it surprising that a loving Creator has in mercy given us both the warnings and the positive encouragements to point us to something better? That something better is marriage, as the Bible depicts it.

Marriage is not an easy option; it needs working at. Some marriages involve great sacrifices and a great burden of suffering. Most are far from ideal. Yet marriage is also a haven and a school for character. Without clear guidelines on marriage we shall never be able to build happy families and stable, creative communities. Here is a challenge and a warning to Christians in Britain today. With open eyes and open Bibles we cannot plead ignorance.

*Note*

*"One flesh"*

The inner meaning of God's gracious gift of marriage to mankind is summarised in the term "one flesh" (Matt. 19 : 4–6). The primary reference of "one flesh" is to the organic union of the two persons, to a new unitary existence, and hence to a complete partnership of man and woman. This is supported by the use of Gen. 2 : 24 in Eph. 5 : 32 as a reference to the organic union between Christ and His church, as well as to husband and wife. The Bible has in mind a social and relational unit of two people who belong to each other in such a way that without each other they are less than themselves; the unity cannot be broken without damage to both partners in it.

The fact that in human relations the "one flesh" interpersonal communion comes into being through (and is maintained by) sexual intercourse, is supported by Paul's use of the phrase to refer to the ghastly parody of marriage enacted between a man and a prostitute in 1 Cor. 6 : 16. The sense of that whole paragraph is of the incongruity of attempting to separate the sexual part of life from total personal commitment. The one is intended to be the expression of the other. Sexual union seals and completes the marriage covenant as an affirmation of exclusive love and of the commitment to parenthood.

In our fallen world no marriage displays the full riches which God has set in human complementarity for our joyful discovery. Many valid marriages fail to claim or to fulfil much of the Divine promise – they are *poor* marriages. But non-consensual sex acts (e.g. rape, seduction of the young or the mentally deficient), casual or mercenary acts of fornication, adulterous, incestuous or homosexual intercourse are all *invalid* unions, diabolical caricatures of the God-given "one flesh" norm. Hence the stern way in which Scripture forbids them.

For further study see *Marriage, Divorce and the Church* (S.P.C.K., 1971) and Paul Ramsey, *One Flesh* (Grove Books, 1975).

CHAPTER THREE

# Motherhood

Everyone who is sane, everyone who feels himself to be a person in the world, and for whom the world means something, every happy person, is in infinite debt to a woman.

So wrote the famed child psychiatrist, the late D. W. Winnicott in his classic study, *The Child, The Family and the Outside World.*[1] This chapter and the next examine the vertical dimension of the family – the generational division within the family which exists as a result of parenthood – becoming and being a mother or a father. We consider first the figure of mother. Perhaps the deepest natural tie of all is that between mother and child. Every human infant was for nine months developing within its mother's body, and therefore totally dependent upon her. What bond could be stronger?

## I

We start our examination of this theme by looking at motherhood in society. The sense in which marriage exists for the family was explained firstly in terms of the need to regulate and render predictable sexual gratification (which might otherwise engender continual conflict, confusion and frustration), and secondly to secure the nurture of the young. Thus every society has anticipated that marriage will result in a family – i.e. that the *procreative* aspect of sexual exchange will be fulfilled as well as the relational enrichment. To quote the American theologian Paul Ramsey: "An act of sexual intercourse is an act of love. But it is also an act of procreation."[2] It has within it the potential of a new individual life, the possibility of a new member of the human community. As Ramsey amplified the link: "Acts which of themselves tend to strengthen the bonds of love also tend to the production of children."[3] This is a simple fact which most societies have taken seriously by regulating sexual availability through marriage. In this way children are guaranteed two members of the adult community to care for them, to attend to their health during the years of dependence and induct them into the life and lore of the society. Mother however stands closest of all to the child. As Rousseau put it in *Emile*: "Point de mère, point d'enfant" – no mother, no child.

In surveying the concept of motherhood in different societies, we have to note a further physical factor which appears to be simply given in the biological structure of man, besides the parental development within the mother's womb already mentioned. This is the factor of lactation. Human females are normally equipped to feed their children from their own bodies after birth; fathers are not so equipped. Despite the advent of successful bottle feeding, the physical indications seem to point to a need, and to the fact that the initial core relation of a family with children is the mother-child attachment,[4] and milk from the mother's breast strengthens this bond. It is mother whom all societies recognise as responsible for bearing and caring in the early months of life. And on this basis the role differences in other, though related, tasks have been erected.

The veteran anthropologist Malinowski has pointed out how at first sight even a primitive native tribe displays to the Western observer a familiar pattern of child care:

> . . . the instinctive foundation of maternal love is clearly traceable in a native society. The expectant mother is interested in her future off-spring, she is absorbed in it from the moment of its birth, and in the carrying out of her social duties of suckling, nursing and tending it, she is supported by strong biological inclinations. In a tribe where there are such practices as infanticide or frequent adoption, the natural innate tendencies of maternal love may become rebelliously subservient to custom and tribal law, but they are never completely stifled or obliterated. In any case, once a child is spared, kept and

nursed by the mother, maternal love grows into a passion. And this passion develops as the mother has to guide, watch over and educate her child, and lasts through life. To this the child responds with an exclusive personal attachment to the mother, and the mutual bond remains one of the strongest sentiments in any human society.[5]

In the same essay he sums up the various and enduring dimensions of motherhood in this way:

Maternity is the most dramatic and spectacular as well as the most obvious fact in the propagation of species. A woman, whether in Mayfair or on a coral island of the Pacific, has to undergo a period of hardship and discomfort; she has to pass through a crisis of pain and danger, she has, in fact, to risk her own life in order to give life to another human being. Her connection with the child, who remains for a long time part of her own body, is intimate and integral. It is associated with physiological effects and strong emotions, it culminates in the crisis of birth, and it extends naturally into lactation.[6]

These quotations are a generalisation, admittedly. Not every woman wants her child desperately, and not every mother adores her new-born child. The affectionless mother, or the mother whose initial love for her offspring is weak or uncertain, is however encouraged by social pressure to *behave* as a loving mother, and in this way love often emerges and grows.

Hence pre-natal as well as post-natal social signs, symbols, taboos and rituals all mark out mother-and-child as a relationship which society wishes to validate and to strengthen in the interests of the welfare of the offspring. The individual bond must be confirmed. The very words "mother", "child", "my child", "son" and "daughter" must all resonate together in a solemn chord in the public as well as the private consciousness.

To quote Malinowski again:

The whole cultural apparatus continues to reaffirm and to reshape the bond of maternity, and to individualise it with force and clearness. These anticipatory moral influences always put the responsibility upon one woman and mark her out as the sociological or cultural mother over and above her physiological claims to that title. . . . We can thus say that motherhood is always individual. It is

never allowed to remain a mere biological fact. Social and cultural
influences always endorse and emphasise the original individuality of
the biological fact. These influences are so strong that in the case of
adoption they may override the biological tie and substitute a
cultural one for it. But statistically speaking, the biological ties are
almost invariably merely reinforced, re-determined and remoulded
by cultural ones.[7]

Clearly society has an interest in publishing and
remembering the fact that *that* mother is the parent of *that*
child.

The contrast with our own society is considerable. While
there is of course a right respect for the privacy of the
family and the individual mother-to-be, social mobility and
isolated, individualised living patterns often mean that few
if any neighbours are conscious that there is a baby on the
way. Close relatives usually know, but they may well be
living some distance away. Birth itself takes place either at
home with professional medical personnel in attendance, or
in a specialised institution (hospital or nursing home), and
we are therefore far less able to structure the event as
unique – which it certainly is for the nuclear family concerned – or as a source of communal thanksgiving and cele-
bration. A visit to the local registrar, and the issue of a
family allowance book are not exactly rich in symbolic and
emotional social significance!

It may be no accident that the comparative poverty of the
social dimension of motherhood has come upon us at the
same time as a number of other developments. Consider the
impact of the mass media legitimation of easy sexual indulgence without any thought of procreation, the publicity
given to widespread fears of world over-population, the
sedulous propagation of the phrase "the unwanted child"
and the ghastly practice of the destruction of unborn
children in the womb. A disturbing expression, all the more
worrying because so easy to pronounce from apparently
compassionate motives, is the phrase "one-parent family".
The phrase is usually used of a child-plus-mother unit where
the father has abandoned the mother and their child. Most

people have an in-built reluctance to accord the word "family" to the tragic figure of an unsupported mother and her child. Furthermore, earlier societies would be bewildered not so much by the fact of children being born out of wedlock (this has been recognised as something which happens in every society) as by the spectacle of a mother isolated, unable or even unwilling to identify the father of her child so as to ensure that he might undertake responsibility, willingly or unwillingly, for the new life which, under God, he had helped to create. *The Finer Report* told us that there were in 1974 over half a million fatherless families in Britain – ten per cent of all families. On May 2nd, 1978 in the House of Lords, the Bishop of Leicester spoke of a quarter of a million children living in one-parent families. And he went on:

> Two hundred thousand children every year now face the trauma of a breaking home. I do not know whether your Lordships heard this morning a little extract on the radio by one of the leaders of the Samaritans talking about little children who are fearing suicide or even hopefully looking forward to it, and who get in touch with the Samaritans. The first explanation given to the radio reporter who was asking, "Why do they do it?" was that "it may be that their homes are breaking up".[8]

The burden of an unsupported mother is heavy and one which no mother ought to have to bear. The compassionate tolerance of Government spokesmen on this issue, and the apparent inability to discern how the whole concept of motherhood is being decisively shifted today by legislation, by the mass media and by the refusal to ensure family-based sex education in schools, is a depressing feature of our contemporary scene.

A good model of motherhood is essential. So much human learning takes place by imitation, conscious or unconscious. The conceptual geography of any society is always changing, including the variety and strength of models available for imitation. At one level Richard Hoggart has described the Northern working-class mother of the inter-war years, and surely of many decades prior to his own period. He painted an unforgettable picture of the figure known as "me mam" in his *Uses of Literacy*.[9] Here again, the pattern had for long been clear. The growing girl was given a good clear model, perhaps not as rich or as varied as might have been wished ideally; but at any rate something clear-cut. The next generation knew what was expected of them. It is certainly not so today. On the broadest level, our contemporary Royal family are a powerful focus of interest and admiration, and we can only be grateful that a clear pattern of family obligations has been set before the nation in the Queen and Prince Philip. Church and political leaders also have their part to play in this respect. But so too, alas, do media figures. A typical, successful TV actress's attitude to marriage and motherhood is not always a positive one, but such a-typical (and often irresponsible) women achieve maximum coverage in the *Radio Times* and the *TV Times* weekly. The weakness and the contradictions of the contemporary, socially-mediated image of woman is significant in this context. As a result we find so many confused expectations in the minds of girls and young people today. This comparatively sudden loss of clarity in the definition of marital roles will certainly affect our concept of motherhood.

In examining any social model of motherhood we begin by noting that a mother is always a woman. Now the pressure today in society is undoubtedly towards what has been called an androgynous culture, which would give little or no acknowledgment to sexual differences. This trend, which tends to reduce sexual differences to a minimum, is marked among intellectuals and in legislation. Its only denial seems, interestingly enough, to emerge in leisure and fantasy occupations such as the over-sexualised world of the pornographers. The pressure towards the abolition of sexual differences was seen markedly at the time of the Communist Revolution earlier this century in the Soviet Union, where it still persists, so that it may be said that this trend exists world-wide. Early Russian Marxist theory even flirted with the possibility of the abolition of the family, but as we have noted, after some years of this experiment it was found that the social dislocation caused by the down-grading of family responsibilities was too much for society to endure. The roles of father and mother, and a certain degree of family loyalty, were brought back. The primacy of the claims of the State over all family loyalties was retained, however, and so was the equality of men and women at work. The result has been pressure put upon Soviet working women to place their children in creches and nursery institutions so that they can compete with men at work in most fields. To the Soviet State this weakening of the early bond between mother and child has the additional advantage of leaving the children in their formative years much more open to political manipulation.

In the free countries of the West, it is largely economic pressures in the capitalist framework which have stressed the great disadvantage in thinking of women primarily as housewives and mothers, rather than as potential workers. Though advertisers persist in using the image of the young attractive housewife and mother in the home to increase consumer spending, it is an ironical result of their success that many a wife is forced out to work in order to obtain the furniture and gadgets of affluence which the "home" of the advertisers has so successfully projected as desirable! Of recent years in this country the trend towards regarding childbirth and children as hindrances to the affluent home, to economic advancement and to female career prospects, has strengthened. To this has been added the querying of all innate psychological differences between the sexes by militant feminists, together with the cult of the aggressive female and (to a somewhat lesser degree) of the effeminate male.

These tendencies may well constitute a serious threat to civilised life as we know it, which can only preserve certain values by the ascription of very clear and different sex roles. One of the strongest statements of this position has come from the American George Gilder. He writes of the systematic degrading of the status of the housewife – that is, woman as mother and homemaker. He redresses the balance thus:

It is foolish to imagine that the complex roles and relationships sustained by the housewife can be abolished or assumed by outside agencies. Her role is nothing less than the central activity of the human community. All the other work – the business and politics and entertainment and service performed in the society – finds its ultimate test in the quality of the home. The home is where we finally and privately live, where we express our individuality, where we display our aesthetic choices, where we make and enjoy love, and where we cultivate our children as individuals. All very pedestrian, perhaps, but there is not very much more in civilised life.

The central position of the woman in the home parallels her central position in all civilised society. Both derive from her necessary role in procreation and from the most primary and inviolable of human ties, the one between mother and child. In those extraordinary circumstances when this tie is broken – as with some disintegrating tribes – broken as well is the human identity of the group. Most of the characteristics we define as humane and individual originate in the mother's love for her children.

Deriving from this love are the other civilising concerns of maternity; the desire for male protection and support, the hope for a stable community life, and the aspiration for a better future. The success or failure of civilised society depends on how well the women can transmit these values to the men, to whom they come less naturally. The woman's sexual life and how she manages it is crucial to this process of male socialisation. The males have no ties to women and children – or to long-term community – so deep or tenacious as the mother's to her child. That is primary in society, all else is contingent and derivative.

This essential female role has become much more sophisticated and refined in the modern world. But its essence is the same. The woman assumes charge of what may be described as the domestic values of the community; its moral, aesthetic, religious, nurturant, social and sexual concerns. In these values consist the ultimate goals of human life; all those matters that we consider of such supreme importance that we do not ascribe a financial worth to them. Paramount is the worth of the human individual, enshrined in the home, and in the connection between a woman and child. These values transcend the market place. In fact, to enter them in commercial traffic is considered a major evil in civilised society; whether one proposes to sell a baby or a body or a religious blessing, one is conscious of a deep moral perversion.

The woman's place in this scheme is deeply individual. She is valued for her uniqueness. Only a specific woman can bear a specific child, and her tie to it is personal and infrangible. When she raises the child she imparts in privacy her own individual values. She can create children who transcend consensus and prefigure the future; children of private singularity rather than "child development policy". Even the husband ultimately validates his individual worth through the woman. He chooses her for her special qualities and she chooses him to submit his marketplace reward to her – and to her individual values. A man in courtship offers not chiefly his work but his indidivuality to the woman. In his entire adult life, it may be only his wife who receives him as a whole human being.

One of the roles of the woman as arbiter, therefore, is to cultivate herself; to fulfil her moral, aesthetic and expressive being as an individual. There is no standard beyond her. She is the vessel of the ultimate values of the society. The society is what she is and what she demands in men. She does her work because it is of primary rather than instrumental value. The woman in the home with her child is the last bastion against the technocratic marketplace.[10]

There is some special pleading, some exaggeration, a certain degree of rhetoric and at least a dash of male chauvinism in Gilder's writing. But there is also considerable truth. And if woman is not certain of the primacy of her affective and expressive function, then undoubtedly the health of motherhood in society will suffer.

## II

We must now say something about motherhood as an individual experience, and its place within the life of the family. The coming of the first child decisively alters the quality and shape of the marriage relationship. Physical changes make it clear to the mother that a baby is "on the way". The husband – for all his love, sympathy, understanding and support – is from now on a spectator of something which is the peculiar, intimate and inalienable business of his wife. Just as he married her in the past because she was a woman – a member of the complementary sex, and delightfully different for that reason (though not for that reason alone) – so now he recognises an experience which he cannot share and which renders her mysteriously different, perhaps even more baffling and challenging. She must bear the child. Hormonal, attitudinal and physical changes are but the chemically and physically measurable aspects of these profound alterations of character, feeling response and sense of duty. The whole emotional tone of the marriage alters.

Expressing this at a more practical level: a new focus of interest for both father and mother comes into being. This is the child who is, and is to be. The inevitably introverted, dyadic relationship of the honeymoon and the early part of married life is now to be re-arranged in the interests of another person, a supremely vulnerable and helpless person, whom both instinct and society will tell the pair is "theirs" in a unique way. What might perhaps have seemed a selfish involvement in each other now becomes in the most natural way possible turned outwards to another member of the community whose insistent needs the couple cannot ignore – "*our* child".

We have noted earlier the cognitive, intellectual world-building enterprise which is constantly going on between the married couple by conversation and inter-change. Children add an extra dimension to the validity and stabilising activity of this reconstruction of reality in the home. Berger and Kellner describe it thus:

> If one conceives of the marital conversation as the principal drama and the two partners as the principal protagonists of the drama, then one can look upon the other individuals involved as the supporting chorus for the central dramatic action. Children, friends, relatives and casual acquaintances all have their part in reinforcing the tenuous structure of the new reality. It goes without saying that the children form the most important part of this supporting chorus. Their very existence is predicated on the maritally established world. The marital partners themselves are in charge of their socialisation *into* this world, which to them has a pre-existent and self-evident character. They are taught from the beginning to speak precisely those lines that lend themselves to a supporting chorus, from their first invocations of "Daddy" and "Mummy" on to their adoption of the parents' ordering and typifying apparatus that now defines their world as well. The marital conversation is now in the process of becoming a family symposium, with the necessary consequence that its objectivations rapidly gain in density, plausibility and durability.[11]

But practical adjustments are demanded as well as emotional and intellectual re-orientations with the advent of a child. Parenthood introduces a completely new and time-consuming responsibility into the marriage, and thus inevitably presents a privilege which inhibits personal freedom, more especially that of the mother. The choice of marriage for a woman must often be what it is not for a man – the choice *against* a career. Some occupations are of course better suited to intermittent and part-time application than others. Much depends on the mother's job, and on the level within the job at which the individual woman has been active or would wish to become active again in the future. But if any woman feels that her family is an unwelcome interruption in the progress of her career, it is likely that her family will suffer from her suppressed resentment.

But why *should* the child come first? Why should we care if in twenty-five years the percentage of married women working has more than doubled? Or that in 1974 nine per cent of mothers of children under five were in full-time employment and seventeen per cent in part-time employment?[12] The reason for this prior claim of the infant child is simply the need to learn to love and be loved. The normal child learns this experience from mother, and from time spent with mother. The oral contact of feeding is supplemented by the constant warmth and support of bodily closeness, a source of pleasure and security of a more diffuse kind. The whole of the first part of Winnicot's well-known work *The Child, The Family and The Outside World* is a leisurely, sensitive and reassuring survey of the process of motherhood in the light of modern knowledge of child development. Essentially Winnicot aimed to give mothers "reliance on their natural tendencies" so that the book, as he puts it, is "about the things a devoted mother does by just being herself".[13] The underlying theme of all his descriptions, explanations and gentle prescriptions is *love*. We may take one example at random. In his simple introduction to the study of infant feeding in chapter four, he writes:

> To go to the root of the matter right away, infant feeding is a matter of infant-mother relationship, a putting into practice of a love-relationship between two human beings.[14]

Winnicot's work is a healthy reaction to the feeling which a generation or two of American mothers have had – that you can't rear a child without having a copy of Dr. Spock (or a similar manual of child care), to which you constantly refer. Winnicot's approach is usually a simple confirmation of what love demands, with a little dash of common sense.

One other area of research into the mother-child relationship should be mentioned. This is the whole matter of maternal deprivation. Investigations have revealed the harmful effect upon the growth of the child's personality which can result from a break in the continuous loving relationship with the mother or mother-substitute. John Bowlby has been the pioneer investigating this field and his book *Child Care and the Growth of Love* has become a classic since it appeared in the early 1950s. The relationship must be warm, intimate and continuous, experienced as satisfying, enjoyable and rewarding on both sides. Up to a certain extreme limit, Bowlby declared, "Young children thrive better in bad homes than in good institutions."[15] Despite some challenges and denials, Bowlby's conclusions have been largely accepted and the concept of maternal deprivation has gained wide currency.

Rutter however in a recent book *Maternal Deprivation Reassessed*[16] has re-examined Bowlby's evidence, together with many subsequent and related studies. He concluded that Bowlby's pioneer work was immensely influential and that it has led to a remarkable change of outlook, followed by a widespread improvement in the institutional care of children. It is now accepted without question that early life experiences may have serious and lasting effects on personal development. And there are clear and undeniable associations between later delinquency and earlier broken homes.

Work is now continuing on the analysis of the whole complex of factors which are to some degree concealed by the term "maternal deprivation", as if it were a unitary cause. There are many factors in normal healthy development: lasting bonds with a known and trusted parent (or as the jargon has it, "care-taker"); the constant stimulus of varied perceptual and linguistic experience; adequate nutrition and a home life free of serious stress. In the light of this ideal pattern one must conclude "take away mother and *normally* you are taking away most of that". But sometimes a child's needs can be successfully met by others, as adoption, foster-parents and so on have shown. Furthermore, it is right to state that an exaggerated, oversimplified and selective picture of Bowlby's findings has rendered some social workers disinclined to rescue children from brutal and psychotic parents and the most appalling home circumstances.[17] Over the last few years we have all heard of examples in news items which the press have not failed to bring before us. It has been discovered since Bowlby's earlier work that physical separation need not always involve the disruption of the bond between parents and child. Distorted relationships rather than weak bonds within the family seem to contribute to anti-social behaviour. Pre-separation experiences also affect the type of impact which the death or departure of the mother may cause.

To be practical, it seems clear that ideally every child needs a loving relationship, leading to an attachment, which is unbroken and which provides adequate stimulation, supplying mothering, and occurring within the child's own family. All these the traditional model of mother can provide. Others can under certain circumstances become mother-surrogates. In extended family patterns, others – especially grandmothers – can take over a considerable portion of this responsibility. But in most societies the traditional pattern of family life, at least for the first three or four years, has ascribed these tasks to mother. Here we have a simple, effective, socially sanctioned and instinctively approved arrangement – motherhood. Without rigid enforcement – for there are always exceptions where responsibilities cannot be met – we should surely be foolish to cease to commend it as the norm for succeeding generations.

### III

We now consider the implications of Christian doctrine for motherhood. As he approaches the Christian revelation to ask what framework of values and priorities is offered on this topic, the intelligent believer who desires to be faithful to the teaching of the Bible is conscious of two particular dangers.

Firstly, he knows how nature worship in pagan cultures has debased human sexuality. This is seen not only in the occurrence of fertility magic, so-called "sacred marriages", prostitute priestesses, complex rituals intended to represent and re-activate the annual rebirth of living things at the spring festival, but also in the deeper symbolism of mythology where ultimate reality (to use our modern desiccated idiom) is pictured as the great Earth-Mother, fruitful and protective but nevertheless, dark, stagnant and devouring. In most pre-literate and some ancient religions, the mother-goddess is dominant. Her son/lover/husband is secondary and derivative, and often he is a mere appendage who is castrated or killed by her. The primacy of the mother-goddess no doubt reflects the basic physiological and anatomical fact that the son comes out of the mother and not vice-versa.[18]

This mythical pattern has further ramifications, since it is a masculine hero who often finally overcomes the chaotic and engulfing force of the Earth-Mother, and some have seen aspects of actual social history mirrored in it. One of the writers in the Anglican report *Women and Holy Orders*, which contains much important psychological material, expresses it thus:

The transition from a society which is dominated by the female to one in which male values are predominant is widely represented in myth and ritual. . . . The male world often only comes into being by an act of forcible emancipation. The myth of the hero who triumphs over the dragon-mother and her dark kingdom is enacted in puberty rites, which involve a dramatisation of separation from the mother and the world of women, a symbolic death with a rebirth from a male-mother, and incorporation into the man's house and the adult male society. As the myths are elaborated, the theme comes to have a more general significance (although this is sometimes evident in myths which might be regarded as most primitive). The triumph of male over female is the victory of masculine light, culture and differentiated consciousness over the feminine womb of water, chaos and darkness. The feminine abyss remains a danger, however; it promises blissful repose, but this means being swallowed and submerged, order and consciousness being lost in chaos.[19]

Whether historically correct or not, there can be little doubt that the ascription of gender in this mythical pattern has been discovered in widely differing ages and cultures and that it has had a profound influence upon the way in which religion and sexuality were linked; upon the actual roles ascribed to the two sexes in the human community and upon the way in which religion has validated a particular view of femininity and motherhood.

It need hardly be said that of this deep and fearful hostility to womanhood there is no hint in Scripture, though faint echoes of the pagan legend can be heard behind the lofty poetry which the book of Job employs when describing the creation; "Rahab" is probably a de-mythologised version of the female chaos-monster who needed to be vanquished so that order and light might prevail (Job 9 : 13, 26 : 12), though in other Old Testament passages the same title Rahab clearly applies to Egypt as vanquished at the Exodus by Jehovah (e.g. Ps. 89:10, Is. 51:9). So Biblical Christianity is, happily, free from the figure of the threatening, universal, engulfiing mother. Time and nature are indeed vast and awesome. In many ways we are dwarfed by the created order. The Christian view is different, as C. S. Lewis so often reminded us. Our faith explains that Nature is not our mother, but our sister.

The second danger as we approach any religious consideration of motherhood arises from the historical fact that one particular mother – acknowledged by all Christians as uniquely and graciously favoured by God – has been raised by a large section of Christendom over the centuries to a position falling not far short of divinity. The cult of Mary has roots which can be traced back to two apocryphal documents of the early centuries of the church, but received its principal stimulus from the great influx of pagans with other Near-Eastern religious backgrounds into the church after Christianity became popular with the conversion of Constantine. The contrast of the pagan mythologies with Christianity (whose Triune God taught His followers to refer to Him in masculine terms) was evident, and the elevation of Mary seemed to provide a needed and familiar female element within, or at least very close to, the divinity.

Eventually in 1854 the Church of Rome declared (the official word is "defined") Mary's Immaculate Conception, and in 1950 her Bodily Assumption into heaven – two events parallel to those in the life of Jesus Himself. Since the Middle Ages, Mary has been referred to as "Our Lady" and as "Queen of Heaven".[20] Though culturally speaking the catholic image of Mary also may well have had a softening and ennobling effect upon many individuals and institutions, it was at the expense of further distancing the compassionate figure of the incarnate Saviour. Nowhere is this theological skew more vividly seen than in the quest of the Augustinian monk Martin Luther in his earnest early years of Bible study seeking for "a gracious God". In those days Christ and even the Father were to him only forbidding figures without a hint of grace, mercy or softness in them. More to the point in our present context is the fact that though Mary as the ideal symbol of motherhood can, and surely did, dignify the concept and experience of motherhood for untold millions, the raising of Mary beyond the status given her in Scripture tended to remove *her* also from the realm of reality. Raised into a transcendent sphere, she too became different from us. Assertions of her miraculous birth and miraculous departure from the world only served to underline this strangeness. And her supposed perpetual virginity showed a Manichean suspicion of sexual experience as specially tainted, a doctrine for which Christianity is so often reproached today, and with some justification.

In fact, Scripture takes *ordinary* motherhood seriously. In the very first chapter of the Bible, we read that having created man in His own image male and female, God commanded them to be fruitful and multiply. This is the family mandate, with its implication of motherhood as an integral part of the process. In the second chapter of Genesis we meet the very first situation in an unfallen creation which was declared to be "not good" – the loneliness of man without woman as helper and companion. Eve was created to meet this need. This deeper unity in their origin is also envisaged as their destiny; Genesis 2: 23 & 24 speaks of Eve specifically as *of* Adam's flesh, but then of marriage as an institution through which man and woman *become* one flesh. At the Fall, child-bearing (though still in the future) becomes charged with ambiguity. Though now fraught with pain and danger, it contained also the hidden promise of a child who should one day bruise the serpent's head. The name "Eve" in fact seems to be connected with Adam's consciousness that her motherhood of all the living had now some special extra significance (Gen. 3 : 20).

A problem which we touched upon in the previous chapter now demands further expansion. What is the exact status of motherhood within the context of marriage, viewed theologically? Is it the main purpose or function, as has often been asserted? Or, at the other extreme, is mother-hood an optional extra? The problem is posed most acutely in our own day because of the widely available means of contraception. Formerly every act of love was in principle a potential act of generation, so that the unitive and the pro-creative functions of sexual exchange seemed indissolubly linked. But contraception has changed all this. The serious health hazards of the contraceptive pill, the failure rate of every known method of contraception – these are important areas of growing knowledge. They should be better known. Clearly, vested interests desire to suppress these facts – as recent cases in Denmark have shown.[21] But the question we are asking is a deeper one: *If* we had a perfect contraceptive – completely safe and completelty reliable – under what circumstances (if at all) would it be right for Christians to use it to avoid motherhood?

The bearing that the question has upon motherhood is obvious. In Scripture parenthood was always a blessing, ever since Eve exclaimed "I have gotten a man with the help of the Lord" (Gen. 4 : 1), and Abraham waited those long years for the promised son. The story of Job shows vividly the favour of God in granting a large and united family of sons and daughters, illustrating the principle of the well-known Psalm 127 that children are a "heritage from the Lord", a reward, a source of joy, a strength and a defence. Negatively the childless wife is seen in Scripture as a sad figure – we remember the bitter laughter of Sarah (Gen. 18 : 12), Rachel's envious desperation (Gen. 30:1), the voiceless prayer of Hannah in the temple (I Sam. 1 : 10) and Elizabeth's joy that God had "taken away her reproach" (Luke 1 : 25). God's covenant love promised in Deuteronomy contained a guarantee that no marriage in Israel would be childless as long as the people were obedient (Deut. 7 : 14). In Scripture therefore marriage without children is at best sad, at worst a sign of God's displeasure. That any godly couple should will this upon themselves is unthinkable. That must therefore be our Christian starting point. We must go on to assert however that the godly couple who are childless through no intention of their own have a valued part to play in any church – they are probably more mobile, more able to offer hospitality and more able to help other families in emergencies – and will in addition very often consider adoption. There is no suggestion in the

New Testament that infertility in a Christian couple is a sign of divine disapproval.

We must also assert that acts of love should not simply be enjoyed without respect to their procreative possibility – thus resulting in the continual series of pregnancies which have so exhausted many a Roman Catholic mother. The tension between a married pair's enjoyment of each other in the "one-flesh relationship" and the procreative possibility of each sexual act is surely rightly resolved by allowing for a distinction but not a total separation between the unitive and the generative aspects of the couple's coming together. Both are essential elements in marriage, but a happy marriage can and should be sustained by far more occasions of physical union than are necessary to produce the possibility of the number of children deemed appropriate or tolerable to the couple. Contraception can resolve this tension, and is thus *in principle* not morally problematic. The twin "goods" of marriage, relation and procreation, are separable and may on many occasions be justifiably separated; God-given control over nature surely includes man's own body and nature as well as his environment, and the Christian should not shirk the task of determining the biblical use of such new means of controlling our own destiny as God has permitted us to discover.

There are however two limiting factors here. The first relates to the particular methods of the control of fertility which may be used. Chemical means are still in their infancy and entail substantial risks. Mechanical means may not be morally dubious, but they are open to objection on aesthetic grounds, besides those of discomfort and inconvenience. "Natural" means seem on the whole appropriate – as well as the most widely used, as a matter of fact. The problems associated with other methods of contraception are summed up by Oliver O'Donovan in this way:

> The fact that contraception is *as such* morally unproblematic should not hide the fact that its widespread use can foster unhealthy attitudes. And that not only by making fornication easier. It is all too

easy for conscientious "planned parents" to forget that their children are still a "gift of the Lord", not summoned into being by parental *fiat*. And certain types of contraceptive method raise special moral problems. Christians could well decide to avoid on principle any that are shown to operate as post-conceptive abortifacients. The use of sterilisation as a method of contraception (i.e. where it is not medically indicated), though free from moral objections in itself, nevertheless raises issues of moral concern. Still for all practical purposes irreversible, sterilisation closes future options decisively; what about widowhood, death of existing children, and so on?[22]

Far more important however is the question which lies at the root of everything we have so far said about family, marriage and motherhood. Contraceptives present to a couple the possibility of entering marriage with the intention of having a full sexual relationship *but also* no family. The intention would therefore be "planned non-parenthood" – a deliberate, total separation of the unitive from the generative, of relation from procreation. Protestants have never felt able to solve this by forbidding all contraceptive practices, nor by setting procreation as the chief or primary good in marriage. Rather it seems from Scripture that the two privileges of marriage, separable as they now are, should never be intentionally *totally* separated, except for some overridingly serious and exceptional reason. The weight of Christian moral tradition is against the deliberately childless marriage except on the weightiest of considerations. The commitment to parenthood is part of the whole commitment to each other which the marriage promise comprehends. The number of children and the spacing of children may well be a matter of conscious deliberation and decision, both before and during the years of married life. But the family is God's pattern and motherhood is a blessing – hence (probably) the somewhat cryptic words of 1 Timothy 2 : 15 about the woman being saved through bearing children. This should be the norm, the duty and the path of obedience as well as of fulfilment for the married woman. Parenthood is not a dimension of marriage which a couple, once married, are free to opt *into*.

Parenthood may, alas, be something which a minority of couples reluctantly opt *out of*.[23]

Motherhood in its other manifold aspects is a constant theme in Scripture. The patriarchal narratives show us the complex web of jealousy in the bigamy of Abraham (Gen. 16) and the divisive factor of twins spoiled – one favoured by mother and the other by father (Gen. 25). Of considerable importance to any study of the place of the mother is the remarkable final chapter of the book of Proverbs. This begins with some proverbial warnings against promiscuity and strong drink from the mother of king Lemuel, and concludes with a wonderful picture of the virtuous wife. She is the mother of children, but is able to act in many respects as the head of the household. She is economically productive, buys and exploits land, weaves and trades in clothes, manages the household, arranges charitable giving and works overtime into the night. Not surprisingly, she is physically strong and her husband profits from and is grateful for her activities. Nothing could be less like the "progressive" caricature of what religion does to relationships – a patriarchal domination of the "chattel wife", or the male chauvinist exploitation, which some extreme writers of today see as characterising the wifely role throughout most of recorded history, cramped as we were by religious bigotry until the days of enlightenment through John Stuart Mill, Germaine Greer and Kate Millet! Proverbs 31 certainly has much to teach us about the rich complexity of the possibilities set before the wife and mother in the plan of God. The hyperactive, aggressive masculine stereotype is a distortion of the husband in Scripture (as we shall see in our next chapter). And even a moderate view of man/woman complementarity must be careful not to squeeze the wife and mother – with the best of intentions – into a passive, socially restricted and unproductive role. There is a household-centred pattern evident in most of the activities listed in Proverbs 31, which means probably that "home-making" in its widest sense is still the unique contribution of the ideal wife. But now that women live longer, and cease child-bearing at an earlier age (with fewer children) a mother's life need not be totally child-centred. Indeed, if a certain type of (false) maternal altruism and possessiveness characterises the early mother-hood years, then when children eventually leave home, there is nothing left and the marriage itself can turn sour. Proverbs 31 shows a healthy variety in mother's activities; there seems to be a lesson here for all periods of married life. Husband, we note, is typically outside, "in the gates . . . among the elders in the land" (v.23) – instru-mentally active, as Talcott Parsons might comment with satisfaction.

In the New Testament we have already seen the dignity and glory of conception and birth in the early chapters of Luke, where the Gospel story begins with the conception of John the Baptist and of Our Lord Himself. Mothers emerge fleetingly, though very individually, in the ministry of Jesus, beseeching him for the health or restoration of their children. Care for his own mother was with Jesus in the moments before his death, as he entrusted Mary to the family of the apostle John (Jn. 19 : 27).

In the New Testament Epistles, though there is a wonderful equality of value between all the baptised – for all are sinners, and all are justified by grace – yet distinctions of sexual complementarity (and hence of function) are not obliterated, neither are age differences between generations. The wives of bishops and deacons are assumed to be mothers, and good mothers at that (1 Tim. 3 : 4,12); all older women are to be exhorted and treated like mothers (1 Tim. 5 : 2). Mothers and grandmothers are not only entitled to respect, but also to support from their children and grandchildren (1 Tim. 5:3–8). The older women have a positive task of teaching and example in the church, training the younger women in their tasks of wife and mother "to love their husbands and children, to be sensible, chaste, domestic, kind and submissive to their

husbands, so that the word of God may not be discredited"
(Titus 2 : 5).

From the very beginning the duties of children towards
their mothers are clear. It is father *and* mother who are to
be honoured and respected, according to the fifth commandment, a duty repeated by Jesus (Matt. 19 : 19) and by Paul
(Eph. 6 : 2). The teaching of mother in the home was to be
attended to, and a son is warned more than once in the
Book of Proverbs not to neglect his mother's teaching (1 : 8;
6:20) nor to despise her (15:20; 23:22; 30:17), for a
foolish son is a sorrow to his mother (10 : 1). Eventually
however the time comes for a child to establish a new
primary loyalty when he or she leaves mother and father to
establish a new family unit. What a blessing it is when such
new families can look back down the paths of motherhood
and thank God for the sincere faith which dwelt first in a
grandmother and then in a mother (2 Tim. 1 : 5), as Paul
reminded Timothy that he could do.

It is no small task to be called, as Christians are today, to
summon people back in school and church (and everywhere
else where we can be heard) to motherhood in this rich and
positive Biblical sense. Motherhood matters. At the
moment the cards seem stacked against us. But we have a
witness to bear to the Christian ideal and we must continue
to make it known. Scripture and experience testify to the
crucial function of motherhood for child, for husband, for
family life . . . and for civilised values. In the face of a wide
variety of false, twisted and destructive messages about the
family, and in particular about motherhood, today's
Christians are called to affirm and to celebrate the value of
motherhood in the name of "the Lord, high above the
heavens", who "gives the barren woman a home, making
her the joyous mother of children". (Ps. 113 : 9)

CHAPTER FOUR

# Fatherhood

In this chapter we shall first consider the role of father in a broad social context, and attempt some generalisations from experience. Then we shall enquire what the characteristic features and problems of the modern father are within the family. Finally we shall examine the Biblical material which we need to take seriously if a genuinely Christian concept of fatherhood is to enrich both our own family life, the society to which we are called to contribute and our own understanding of the God who teaches us to call Him "Father".

## I

"There is a sense in which we can take for granted the fact that the mother-child relationship will be a close one in any society," wrote Raymond Smith in his study of *The Negro Family in British Guyana* (1956) "and the real problem then begins to centre on the way in which masculine roles are integrated into the family system."[1] The allocation of tasks in relation to children is the given factor which from the start shapes the asymmetrical distribution of activities within the family. As another sociologist puts it: "The biological nature of the mother-child bond ordinarily leads the mother to perform tasks connected with the child, particularly when it is small, and the father to perform (frequently away from the home) activities that, directly or indirectly, will produce the needed goods and services."[2] And this of course leads to other incidental duties as well.

But why should *this* man perform this task, or any other task for that matter, for *this* particular woman? Here we find a universal social need, and consequently a universal social awareness, that there must be communal conventions, sanctions and celebrations which ensure that a man who has fathered a child may be identified – and indeed may identify himself – as father, and that he is encouraged to say, "This is my child". Thereby he commits himself to the minimal responsibilities of care, protection and provision which guarantee the continuation of the species. In this way we discover cultural compensation everywhere for an inherently weaker bond. Kingsley Davies analysed the position thus:

> The weak link in the family group is the father-child bond. There is no necessary association and no easy means of identification between these two as there is between mother and child. In the reproductive groups of monkeys and apes, the male parent is held in the group, not by any interest in the offspring, by his interest in the female. Among human beings, a bond is created between the father and his children by a complex set of folkways, mores and laws. Similarly, a durable relation is created between him and the mother. The mother's relation to the child is also socially regulated, but in this case the bond is more easily established and maintained.[3]

It is this inherent weakness at the beginning of the father-child bond which demands a strong clear social definition of fatherhood. The veteran anthropologist Malinowski called this definition "the principle of legitimacy". He expressed it in this way:

> What about the father? As far as his biological role is concerned he might well be treated as a drone. His task is to impregnate the female and then to disappear. And yet in all human societies the father is regarded by tradition as indispensable. The woman has to be married before she is allowed legitimately to conceive. Roughly speaking, an unmarried mother is under a ban, a fatherless child is a bastard. This is by no means only a European or Christian prejudice; it is the attitude found amongst most barbarous and savage people as well . . . The most important moral and legal rule concerning the physiological side of kinship is that no child should be brought into the world without a man – and one man at that – assuming the role of sociological father, that is, guardian and protector, the male link between the child and the rest of the community . . . I think that this generalisation amounts to a universal sociological law and as such I have called it . . . the *Principle of Legitimacy*. The form which the

principle of legitimacy assumes varies according to the laxity or stringency which obtains regarding prenuptial intercourse . . . Yet, through all these variations there runs the rule that the father is indispensable for the full sociological status of the child as well as of its mother, that the group consisting of a woman and her offspring is sociologically incomplete and illegitimate. The father, in other words, is necessary for the full legal status of the family.[4]

Now this public recognition of paternity which is so essential for the protection of mother and child, for family stability and for social continuity, is also the basis of other processes and transactions, visible and invisible, in most societies. Once kinship is established and lineage is a public fact, matters such as inheritance arise. A father is expected in normal circumstances to transmit wealth and property to *his* children, in preference to anyone else's. This is a logical extension of the acknowledged duty to care and provide within the family.

A wider concept however is that of status. By virtue of belonging to a particular family with specific position, power and prestige within the community, the child at birth enters a specific status level. And here again, it is normally the father who determines status. The illegitimate child is not entitled to certain benefits and privileges because his father is not known or will not acknowledge him. His status is lost or uncertain; his social identity is problematic. Admittedly he can achieve power and influence in adult life by virtue of exceptional effort or inherited ability, or fortuitous opportunities grasped, or patronage, or more usually a combination of two or more of these. But he starts from nothing as no other child does. Adoption can restore to him an acknowledged starting point, for as Coser comments: "The institution of adoption demonstrates that it is the *social father* who assigns status to the children that are said to belong to his family, whether the father or both parents are physiological agents or not."[5]

In a fascinating study of the way in which the principle of legitimacy is deliberately abandoned in social revolutions, Coser and Coser have explained how utopian social engineers perceive the need to abolish the transmission of all ascribed status differences. Family-determined status is an obvious hindrance to the transformation of class relationships. Hence they immediately "attempt to remove the legal disabilities and moral stigmata that had previously been attached to bastards ... to eradicate the distinctions between persons born in legitimate and those born in non-sanctioned unions".[6] Yet during both French and Russian revolutions, the new freedom and equality did not last long. A new status order inevitably arose. Blood proved to be thicker than even the clear water of the new egalitarian constitution, family stability was found to be permanently satisfying and socially necessary . . . and the principle of legitimacy returned.

This leads us to emphasise the more general point about the role of the father. The family and the home being what they are – and *must* be – the father is inescapably the mediator between family and society. More especially between family and wider status and structures of class, occupation and economic potential. The words of Talcott Parsons usefully summarise the way sociologists view the role of the father in modern society:

> In a certain sense the most fundamental basis of the family's status is the occupational status of the husband and father. As has been pointed out, this is a status occupied by an individual by virtue of his individual qualities and achievements. But both directly and indirectly, more than any other single factor, it determines the status of the family in the social structure, directly because of the symbolic significance of the office or occupation as a symbol of prestige, indirectly because as the principal source of family income it determines the standard of living of the family.[7]

This underlying problem of status presses in very differently upon husband and wife however. The modern urban family is under stress at this point, since the wife is nearly always deprived of the possibility of being an occupational helper and partner in a common enterprise with her husband. Yet with the emphasis upon a significant achievement in a competitive world as the criterion of success or significance, the occupation of "housewife" is devalued. The social priority which assigns to woman the ascribed role of family care, home-making and the less tangible expressive activities, gives women less than full status in the occupational sphere – a frustrating factor to many women today. The Christian may well see the link "occupation = pay = power = status" as a pervasive and poisonous kind of materialism, but when the scent of mammon pervades the network of social assumptions within which life must be lived, an outlook completely free of its taint cannot be easily achieved, even by the Christian. Furthermore the husband's task is typically outside the home, increasingly specialised and therefore less intelligible to his wife and children – and if he is at all aspiring, it represents an increasing drain upon his energy and concentration. This narrows the opportunity for interchange, and the range of common interests husband and wife can share. Again, a husband's career gives him a certain stability despite changes of employer (moving from one employer to another within a certain range of activities, well known to him); the wife however must be prepared for the upheaval of moves and for what one writer has called "the domesticity of transiency". For the woman this means uprooting without any kind of continuity. These are factors which many of today's husbands, Christians included, have not fully taken into account. The vast majority of married women over thirty in Britain today are on tranquillisers.

The allocation of tasks within the family has been the focus of intense and continuous study, particularly since the second World War. The war brought a greater percentage of women into full-time occupations, and after the war the numbers did not seriously decrease. Social analysts developed a great interest in studying the effects of women at work outside the home upon children's development, upon spending patterns and upon family relationships and attitudes.

We need to remember that as an operative system any small group is faced with allocation problems. And much is known about how this process of allocation takes place. Every group needs what is called a "task leader" who suggests courses of action; directs the shared energies of the group; acts as a spokesman; facilitates his or her own performance by the inhibition of emotions, accepts hostility and so on. These are known as *instrumental* activities, ways of ensuring that the group manipulates the object world, or environment, to achieve desired goals. On the other hand, the group also has a need to engage in integrative or *expressive* behaviour – to reinforce its own bonds, to give and receive encouragement and comfort; to laugh, play, show affection, develop an atmosphere of warm and supportive acceptance.

Now the family is a group whose very survival depends on both these two broad categories of experience and activity being provided. From the beginning the group has needed food, shelter, fire and protection, as well as special care for new recruits on the one hand, and the more diffused, integrative contribution to its harmony and stability on the other. It is the father who has in all societies been entrusted with the former responsibilities: the instrumental task. Morris Zelditch has summarised the ideal-typical pattern of this kind of allocation of duties thus:

> The allocation of the instrumental leadership to the husband-father rests on two aspects of this role. The role involves, first, a manipulation of the external environment, and consequently a good deal of physical mobility. The concentration of the mother on the child precludes a primacy of her attention in this direction although she always performs some instrumental tasks. In addition to the managerial aspects of the role, there are certain discipline and control functions of the father role. Consider, again, why *two* parents are necessary at all. The initial mother-child sub-system can do without the father (except that he provides food, shelter, etc. for this sub-system so that it need not split up to perform many of its own instrumental tasks). But some significant member of the nuclear family must "pry the child loose" from the mother-dependency so that it may "grow up" and accept its responsibilities as an "adult". There is necessarily a coalition of father and mother in this, or no stable socialisation pattern develops.[8]

But coalition or no, it is clear that this pattern gives a leading or dominant role to the father. It is of course true that in English working-class culture (as with American middle-class matriarchs) mother has been accorded the status of final arbiter in many aspects of family life. To this extent father's role as "head" or ultimate authority, is diminished, and the distinctions made above have been decisively modified. It is interesting in this connection that the family therapists of the 1970s stress the need for a certain hierarchical order if the family group is to function effectively. Much therapy is faced with the obvious distress caused by a breakdown of control, abdication of responsibility and absence of authority. Robin Skynner has concluded that "families operate best where each parent respects the other and shares responsibility, but where the father is accorded ultimate authority".[9]

It is not suggested that this position does not expose the father to stress. Talcott Parsons and Fox have observed: "The husband/father as the provider and primary status-bearer of the family is exposed during all the working hours of his existence to the distinctive rigours of the market place, wherein he carries the heavy load of responsibility for the family. In addition he is classically a 'scapegoat'; the symbolic target at which the child primarily aims the hostile-aggressive impulses aroused in him as he undergoes the stressful process of socialisation."[10] Such new vistas lead us naturally to a closer consideration of the deeper levels of family interaction.

## II

Much light has been shed on the place of the father in the internal dynamics of the family by work in the areas of individual psychology and psychoanalysis over the past fifty years. We must note at the outset the deliberate boundary in the modern world between job and home – production and consumption, the occupational and the domestic spheres. In one scene, family relationships are irrelevant, at least in theory. In the other they are everything. This duality is built into the experience of the vast majority of working husbands and fathers. The occupational world is one of clearly limited responsibility and authority, and individual merit is measured by competence and performance; in the home, responsibility boundaries are blurred. In practice, business and other occupational organisations have found that they ignore the personal relationships in working teams to their cost. There are emotional factors in all co-operative enterprises, however bureaucratic. Nevertheless domestic patterns of activity are to a greater degree unpredictable and emotionally charged, rather than rational, bureaucratic and planned; children are cared for on the basis of who they are rather than what they can do, and so on. It is the husband's task to switch between these two worlds, and not always without difficulty.

When the child enters this scene at birth, his needs are clear to mother, who at first glance provides them all. Winnicott delays until chapter 17 (page 113) of *The Child, The Family and the Outside World* before asking the question "What about the Father?" He explains the function of father as the focus of those qualities of strength, order and strictness which the infant first discerns in mother, and which are felt to be dissonant with her fundamental softness and sweetness. Because they are not essentially part of her, these "harder" qualities are grouped together in the infant's mind and drawn towards those feelings he is willing to have towards father. A strong father, both respected and loved, a real person, a positive lively personality, is the proper figure to take over these feelings from the mother. Thus father comes to be "the human being who stands for the law and order which mother plants in the life of the child".[11] Father supports and strengthens mother emotionally and morally, opens the wider world of work and society to the child, and sometimes when the child is resentful or angry, he can be the passing object of hatred while mother can be felt as remaining loving.

This is of course an ideal – typical stereotype. Circumstances and temperament can change the model quite substantially in an individual case. The hyper-active, aggressive mother, strongly work-oriented or ambitious, may find a *modus vivendi* as a mother if her husband is able to provide more time and affection for the children than in the average family. But these unusual cases often raise serious problems, especially where mother is seen by others and by the children to "rule the roost".

Another experienced child psychiatrist, Dr. Louise Eickhoff, has expressed the father's contribution in this way (and not without a real poetry of expression):

> Father "speaks" another language, of hard muscles and hairy feel, of earth-shaking unaccustomed vibrations, and a different scent that has no link with home. The home scent and feeling, and the love flow and therefore the chance of life are engendered in the mother whose face becomes the dial from which the child reads life. Everything she does she does differently from her masculine partner, even pram-pushing.
>
> But the child in intimate contact with the mother, warmed by her presence, responding to her lively lap and face, understanding so easily what she "tells him", grows daily in knowledge of this life-necessary giant, this love, and grasps eagerly anything associated with her. So he very easily adds to his impression of her, the strange scent and rich exciting vibrations of the father, remote from him but related to the mother. He unites the two in a composite immensity, mother-faced father-backed and based, the parent complex that is the rock on which life is built, the great tap-root through which life and love will pass for all time, ever growing and rendering more firm, the life dependent upon it.[12]

The basic differentiation which is felt in these earliest weeks of life becomes more deeply apprehended and objectified in a value system as the child grows up. Freud saw human morality as an internalised system made up within the individual from repressed instincts and the authoritative, judgmental and punitive aspects of his parents. The technical psycho-analytic description of this process asserts that the super-ego is constituted by introjected parental values, and is the ultimate, significant factor in character

building. Briefly – and very roughly – the roots of conscience (unconscious moral convictions or presuppositions)
are what the power of the father leaves behind.[13] If there is
more than a shred of truth in this theory – and the greater
part of the psychiatric world would say that there certainly
was – then father-deprivation of any kind leaves a serious
gap. There is ample evidence that serious thinkers are
beginning to recognise this. Dr. Benjamin Spock's book of
"second thoughts", which came out in 1974, paints a
sensitive picture of how things can go wrong in this field.

> More common in America today is the father who is a great pal to his
> son and still leaves all the disciplining to the mother. He may say that
> he doesn't want his son to resent him the way he sometimes resented
> his own father. You get a sense in some such families that the father
> feels like one of the children. He cheerfully ignores the little crises
> that arise all the time in any family, and when his wife realises what is
> going on and begs him to take over some of the control when he's at
> home, or at least to back her up firmly, he does it all too
> half-heartedly to have much effect. Or he gives some excuse he's too
> tired from working all day, or he doesn't want to come home at the
> end of the day and be the ogre. In some of these families, the father
> without realising it is in league with the children, and is subtly
> working against the mother's authority, but in a teasing or
> absent-minded manner. This reluctance of the father to be a
> disciplinarian is just as important a problem as that of the father who
> never plays with his children. It doesn't bother his children – they
> think it's fine. But it bothers the mother. It may be passed on to the
> sons and it will bother the sons' wives. It is part of a broader
> problem: the tendency in a fair proportion of American families for
> the husband to act somewhat like a son to his wife, and for the wife to
> act a mother to her husband. Both attitudes are aspects of the same
> disturbance which is being transmitted through daughters as well as
> through sons.[14]

A little later Spock asks: "What do sons need from their
fathers?" and he answers his own question in words which
show an interesting move back to a more traditional and
even authoritarian pattern:

> It isn't enough for a father to be a pal. A boy should be able to find
> many pals but he has only one father. He needs to feel the strength of
> his father and to have respect for his father as an older more

authoritative person. He is even expected in nature's scheme of things, I think to feel at least a little bit of awe for his father. When a father denies his son these aspects of himself because he's afraid to be anything but a pal it gets the boy's deeper instincts somewhat tangled up inside. He may grow up to be a very agreeable person and a good citizen, but he will fail to give his wife the support she needs and he will set a weak pattern for his son to follow.[15]

What Spock hints at here is the necessity of a model; for these things are transmitted by imitation. He is only voicing the awareness of a deep human need in the growing youngster which is acknowledged by virtually every school of psychology today. Maccoby, for example, in a 1958 study of the effects of the absence of working mothers from home, regarded it as axiomatic even in those days that "for healthy development, the boy needs a strong, masculine model".[16] Brim, in the same year, wrote of the fact that "in families where the father is absent, the male child is slower to develop male sex-role traits than in families where the father is present",[17] though it is stressed that the father-son interaction needs to be warm, affectionate and rewarding. Eickhoff, too points out that though the father is not always around, as the mother is, this need not detract from his special contribution. Though the absentee father (golf-club, politics, religious meetings, bridge, the local "pub", etc.) is not being erected as an ideal, it should be stressed that what matters is what he is and does when he *is* present. He must be strong and he must be different. She writes as follows:

Father poverty undermines the security of the child and its ability to face the unknown or great excitement with that optimistic confidence of a safe landing natural to the well fathered child. All new things including learning, all creations, examinations, class and other changes are exciting in childhood, but are least easily borne when the background is father deficient. Father extends the horizons of his child. Not only by carrying him shoulder high but by being less in the picture than mother. Being therefore, the special bit of the parent complex, the thrill of emphasis, the treat, who can do things impossible for mother to perform. Custom, easy access, sharing the maternal role depreciates his value. But blessed is the father whose wife's dependence upon him and love of him is apparent to the child who sees little of him. His value to the child is the richest endowment policy, enabling the child to feel superior to his fellows, confident of a good backing and of ultimate success. And nothing succeeds like the feeling of success.[18]

Bettelheim and Sylvester have shown[19] how the child's perception of the father's occupation is crucial for the child since it is recognised as the source of the family's livelihood, the reason for father's absence (which the child may construe in all sorts of magical and mysterious ways) and the way in which the parent gains an image of power, status and prestige in the child's eyes. If there is little communication, and as a result a common conceptual world shared by father and child fails to take shape, the whole of the external reality can take on the aspect of an unpredictable, capricious system, manageable – if at all – by some species of magical manipulation.

We have already mentioned the father as scapegoat and the fact that he is rightly to some degree aloof and removed compared with the mother. Philip Slater warns however that although traditionally – e.g. in the Victorian household – aloofness assisted the disciplinary function and was a mechanism for handling hostility, yet the mother tends under these conditions to be seen more as mediator. "She may compensate for her inferior status and power in the society at large by using her strategic position as a mediator to control family relationships."[20] The end-product of this trend is certainly undesirable. Slater describes it thus: "By a combination of public endorsement and private subversion of the father's authority, she indicates to the child that the father is the source of all discomfort and she is the source of all good."[21] That is the way differentiated family roles can become a burden and a source of confusion.

Mention of discipline leads us to consider the topic of punishment. At least in the case of serious offences, punishment normally remains the province of the father, as head of the household, to determine if not to administer. Here again there are traditional class differences in English society; middle class parents use verbal disapproval and withdrawal of affection more frequently, while working class parents go more readily for corporal punishment like a slap or a cuff to the nearest ear. Whatever the method used, it is well-known that the factor of inconsistency or unpredictability is the most dangerous factor to a child's development and a sign of an inadequate parent. In working-class families punishment is more often administered by mothers too.

Maccoby has pointed out how different the effects of punishment can be, depending upon the relationship with the punisher. And this will apply in a very special way to the father when he is called upon to administer punishment.

> Punishment emanating from an individual whom the child does not love leads to fear and efforts upon the part of the child to escape or to conceal his misdeeds from the punisher. Punishment from a loved person, however, creates a different kind of problem for the child, for he wants the affection and approval of the disciplinarian, and he cannot get it by running away. He can only get it by conforming to the demands of the disciplinarian, or, if he does deviate from these demands, by confessing and being forgiven or by repairing the damage he has done. Ultimately, discipline administered by a loved agent is more conducive to the child's "internalising" (accepting as his own) the values being taught him, so that he begins to enforce them upon himself without the continued need of outside discipline.[22]

It should not need to be emphasised that both parents will be agreed on the nature and extent of punitive sanctions in a properly integrated family. Differences of opinion can lead to resentment, needless stress and intra-family feuds and plots. In the pathology of disturbed families containing schizophrenics, a particularly malignant feature of the marriages studied is often the chronic undercutting of the worth of one partner to the children by the other. There is a prominent tendency to compete for the children's loyalty and affection, perhaps in some cases to obtain a substitute who will replace the affection missing from the spouse. But sometimes the intention seems to be simply to hurt the other partner. No parent should ever *wholly* enjoy administering punishment (if he does there may well be an element of sadism or personal vindictiveness present) but the learning of responsibility by the child means the teaching of accountability – i.e. liability to punishment for the transgression of known family "rules". Parents punish because they love, and discipline is part of child care. So there must be harmony between parents in this field, particularly at times when punishment and sanctions are determined and administered.

Much of the research on father-models and father-identification has been done with middle-class subjects. To do justice to other (though perhaps less influential) strata we would need to take into account studies such as Young & Willmott's *Family & Kinship in East London*.[23] Traditional working-class neighbourhoods have preserved much of human value which middle-class insularity has lost. There has been no space to examine these features here. The topic of status is important however, and it emerged in the All Souls' seminar at Oxford convened by Sir Keith Joseph in April 1973. Dr. Esther Goody pointed out the problems of the working-class boy as far as his relationship with his father was concerned:

> An upwardly mobile working-class boy is in a much more difficult position so far as parental status placement is concerned. He wants to break with his father's status, not replicate it, so the father is an embarrassment rather than a help. It might seem that a working-class father had more to contribute to the status placement of a son who is not upwardly mobile. But just what does such a father have to give his son in the way of status? If the family has moved about there will be no position in the community to pass on; financially and occupationally the son can hope to do at least as well as his father without his help. When we look at the situation of a father who is "deprived" – perhaps physically or mentally handicapped, or chronically out of work – his status is a negative quantity which his son can only despise, not hope to emulate.[24]

As far as actively sponsoring his son, again the working-class father is disadvantaged in contrast to the middle-class father. Dr. Goody concludes as follows:

> Perhaps it will now be clear why I think that being an effective adult is so important for successful fatherhood in our society. If fatherhood has few clear functions contributing neither to training for role skills, nor to status placement, nor yet to sponsorship into full adulthood, the importance of the father as a role model is proportionally exaggerated. If the modern working-class father cannot *do* very much for his son, then what he *is* becomes all the more important, because about the only thing he gives his son is an example of how to be an adult.[25]

Like most abstract analyses, this is probably somewhat over-simplified. But it has an obvious message to those of us concerned with character, moral values, and the quality of relationships in society. What messages do children receive daily about "how to be an adult"? One aspect of this loss of status studied by Bakke in the 1930s was the impact of unemployment on the family, and particularly in the way it devalues the husband, engenders resentment and conflict between husband and wife and children, and can produce what Bakke described as an "emergency-dominated energy-consuming and failure-charged atmosphere".[26] This must surely still be a valid comment on the impact of unemployment on many families.

One final element which can weaken positive fatherhood must be mentioned. In a well known essay in the *American Sociological Review*[26] Arnold Green reported the results of his studies of the middle-class male child and neurosis. He concluded that the attitude of the middle-class father in Western industrialised society put children at risk. What he discovered was probably more applicable to America than to this country, but it is worth noting. He drew attention to the mental set of the mobile, competitive, manipulative, career-orientated father. In contrast to the more settled, agricultural pattern of life, the small child with this sort of father would not soon be earning or contributing to the household economy. He would not necessarily be a guarantee of future support in his parents' old age, since in

Western societies today the nuclear family finds it difficult to extend its frontiers of duty and affection beyond the two generations which are its fundamental constitution. Instead, to the aspiring young father his child may well represent a diversion of energy and of funds from (for example) further study for advanced qualifications, courses to increase professional or commercial competence, the entertaining of occupationally advantageous guests and the purchase of the requisite commodities indicating to the wider world a degree of occupational success and a status *just one step ahead* of the point he has actually reached. An exaggerated picture today, perhaps, and possibly less prevalent in the wake of the widespread youth culture revolt of the 1960s against the crasser forms of materialism and the "rat-race" pursuit of professional advancement. Yet even today a child may be seen as an intrusion upon father's devotion to his career. "A certain degree of ambivalence directed towards the child is inevitable,"[28] commented Professor Green, more than thirty years ago. The only new factor today is that mother may provide an echo and an amplification of this feeling, since she too is far more likely to have a career outside the home with financial, if not status, implications.

## III

We begin our Christian approach to father's position with a brief glance at the masculine and father role in other religions. This is not because our faith is derived in linear or evolutionary fashion from any earlier set of beliefs of assumptions (apart from the pure Judaism of the Old Testament), nor because it was hacked out of recalcitrant pagan material by brilliant guesswork on the part of a few inspired moralists, who got some answers right and some wrong, needing later correction by men with deeper insight or more perfect obedience to the still small voice of God as he tried to speak to them. No, we begin with other faiths because the Biblical writers were surrounded by them, and felt their pressure. They were conscious that the faith of Israel was distinct – its characteristic affirmations involved denials of other men's gods. Yet at the same time, the guessings and gropings of other religions only pointed to the needs which all men, as created beings, experienced for a transcendental reference, a cosmic purpose, a personal meaning and an existential direction for living. Because man is a sinner, the light of nature, reason and conscience will be distorted when we survey human experience outside the area illuminated by special revelation – beyond, that is, the confines of Israel and of Holy Scripture. But there will be flashes of insight, true apprehensions of goodness and truth amid the grotesque, cruel and mis-shapen visions of the pagan faiths. Where these are found, they can and should be welcomed. They may sometimes point us to a better understanding of the supreme adequacy of our own faith and to the almost unbearable obligation laid upon us by our privileged position as guardians and servants of a revelation fulfilled and finished in Christ. And just as we have previously discerned in other religious traditions two dimensions of motherhood which were deeply suggestive but not fully Biblical, so there are two aspects of fatherhood which deserve mention in roughly the same context.

The first is the mythical concept of the masculine principle embodied in a god of light, order and specific aggression who triumphs over the (often more ancient) female goddess of darkness, warmth, chaos and un-being. Furthermore, "in most developed mythologies the male god tends to have sterner qualities as ruler, law giver, judge, protector, conqueror and is associated with the sky and with culture".[29] It must be said at once that however much this pattern may echo a deep understanding of the psychic polarity between the disposition and attitudes discovered to be the specific contribution of man and of woman in family and society, the extension of this differentiation into the pantheon has no biblical warrant. Israel *could* have had a female sovereign deity; the persons of the Holy Trinity *could* have contained one or more Persons about whom we could speak using female gender – but in point of fact these things did not happen. God chose to teach His people otherwise. In the light of revelation the pagan mythologies teach us more about human beings than they do about our Creator. They reflect some truth about ourselves, but less truth about God. This is precisely what we should expect in view of the constant tendency of sinful humanity to make God in our own image – to change His glory into something familiar, something we can handle more easily – in plain words, idolatry. We must adore God as He is and as He reveals Himself to be.

There is however a second tendency, a religious "skew" latent in Judaism itself and fully developed in Islam. This is the blazing, oppressive, dynamic, ultra-masculine character of Allah – the one true God to the Muslim. Springing from a Near Eastern and Jewish environment, but rejecting the deity of Christ and the Trinitarian nature of God, the Prophet proclaimed a God characterised by a crushing sense of "otherness". In contemplating this God we are overwhelmed by a consciousness of undifferentiated *power* which swallows up the truly personal, relational aspect known to Christians when they speak of God as Father. The spread of this unitarian ethical monotheism is an impressive cultural achievement. But the ninety-nine attributes and names of Allah do not include love, and the impenetrable unity of the nature of the divine Being demands only submission – a fatalistic acceptance of all events, as man bows before the incomprehensible. This dominant theocratic creed can be seen as hyper-masculinity projected into the image of God – a new idolatry once more. And it is not surprising therefore to find that in countries where Islam's teaching has deeply influenced laws and conventions, the status of woman is very low. Professor Anderson indeed has spoken of the "degradation of Muslim womanhood".[30] Nor are we surprised to discover in Islam's teaching the doctrine of the Jihad or holy war – another manifestation of religiously sanctioned ultra-aggressiveness.

From these aspects of other religions it will be seen that while the masculine element has been the most positive and dynamic, in that the most powerful and most creative cultures have worshipped a male deity (either alone or as chief of a pantheon), certain unsolved problems remain. In remotest antiquity the Aryans' Creator-God was even called Dyaus-Pitar[31] – "Divine Father" – but over time his relation to the world and to man was subject to constant stress and distortion. Wherever we emphasise his unique transcendence, love disappears. Where we introduce plurality and give him a female consort, a proliferation of deities ensues – the well known confusion of mythological polytheism as recorded amongst the Aryans, Egyptians, Greeks, Romans and later cultures.

At least some of these puzzles can be resolved when we turn to the Bible. Our first step is an important one, although not as decisive as some would have us believe. It is to state that the Bible teaches us to speak of God as masculine. This must mean that, despite the option of two personal genders, it is more appropriate to speak of God as male than as female if we have to choose. And we *do* have to choose, since the Creator is personal and teaches us to speak of and to Him personally. Let us at once admit that appropriateness does not indicate adequacy. Ultimately no words are adequate – just as no pictures are adequate to describe the Lord. But while material pictures are forbidden, words relating to human beings and their functions are not; on the contrary, they are necessary. And Scripture enjoins us to use masculine pronouns of the great Creator and Ruler whom we worship.

This must imply that in the male/female polarity which has characterised every culture, it is that much nearer to the truth to see the Lord as the perfection of all that is dimly seen in the conquering warrior, the protecting provider, the ruler and the law-giver than if we had been taught to use the feminine gender with its perennial echoes of a different mode of living and being. The Christian will add to this fact the remarkable additional discovery that all three Persons of the Holy Trinity are unalterably masculine (despite some strange speculations of Canon Demant in an otherwise excellent essay in *Women and Holy Orders*[32]). The pronouns of the Old Testament are underscored by the arrival of God incarnate as Mary's Son and by the coming of the Holy Spirit as the self-effacing but again, unmistakably masculine Counsellor or Advocate.

But theological male chauvinism is not being let loose. We must recall that male and female polarity is not the same as male and female exclusive differentiation. Along the psychological dimensions – attitudinal and personality traits, cognitive and affective abilities – some (though few) women are always more "masculine" than most men, or the average for men, just as some (though few) men are well above the female average into the top-scoring bracket for "womanly" qualities. Outstanding Old Testament women leaders are exceptional – but they are there in the record for our instruction. Theologically, these empirical facts are related to the biblical teaching that man and woman *together* are made in the image of God (Gen. 1 : 27). There is an incompleteness of male without female, of Adam without Eve, as Genesis 2 makes clear. As Professor Torrance has put it, summing up Calvin's doctrine of man and woman: "God created Eve out of Adam in such a way that the two should be one, and that each should be incomplete without the other, and that the two together might cultivate mutual society between themselves."[33]

There are two aspects of this image doctrine. One is related to plurality and order – in this respect the man–woman relationship, being the distinction of persons which makes for human love between man and wife, hints both at the eternal mutual delight in each other enjoyed by the three Persons of the Godhead, and also at the element of government, that loving headship of husband over wife which is analogous both to the relation of the Father to

Jesus, as well as that of God to man.

The other aspect of the image doctrine, is that, in so far as there are positive moral qualities which are ascribed exclusively or more frequently to women, as being more deeply rooted in the female psychic constitution, but which are at the same time necessary for a full and complete expression of humanity (in addition to those which cluster round the masculine pole of our created complementarity), these too must be seen as part of the Divine image, and therefore as part of the perfection of the Godhead. For this reason, any projection of excessively or exclusively masculine stereotypes on to the Being of God must be avoided. A careful reading of Scripture should in any case remind us of the beauty, the tender yearning, the long-suffering and the many other excellencies ascribed to the Divine nature which we tend to associate more with women than with men. It is in this light that we must consider the fact that Jesus did not experience one important part of human life, namely marriage and parenthood. It is not only that the Church is His Bride, the object of His love and affection, but that had He married an earthly wife He would have manifested the masculine but not the complete nature of God, who comprehends more than the masculine – even masculine perfection. These facts then must be set beside the masculinity of God in our theology.

But the masculine theme returns again at another level when man calls God "Father", as he has tentatively done in all the great monotheistic religions, and as we are taught to do in Scripture. The earlier references to the divine Fatherhood in Scripture are found in a creation setting, but later they become more and more charged with meaning. When Israel had become a people after the deliverance from Egypt, the dying Moses taught her to think of Jehovah as "your Father who created you" (Deut. 32 : 6), just as he had earlier reminded them "how the Lord your God bore you, as a man bears his son, in all the way that you want" (Deut. 1 : 31). The same simile – as yet it is no more than a simile – occurs in Psalm 103. "As a father pities his children, so the Lord pities those who fear him" (v.13). Only in the lofty poetry of Isaiah 63 does the simile twice become a symbolic affirmation, the powerful image of a deep reality which can be expressed in no other way. In what has been called one of the most eloquent intercessions of the Bible comes the cry:

> For thou art our Father,
> Though Abraham does not know us
> And Israel does not acknowledge us.

In Malachi (1 : 6, 2 : 10), creation is the relationship under review when the term Father is used, but in Jeremiah (31 : 9) God again speaks of himself as a father to Israel in the warmer, richer context of redemption. However, as with so many other disclosures of the mind of God and His purposes, the New Testament throws a fresh and glorious flood of light upon this motif of God's Fatherhood. Though still used as the title of the One God as Creator (for example in 1 Cor. 8 : 6 and in titles such as "the Father of spirits" (Heb. 12 : 9) or "the Father of lights" (Jas. 1 : 18)), the concept now takes on a new and unprecedented richness in two different, though related, dimensions.

The first is the unique relationship now revealed between the first and second Persons within the triune Godhead, expressed by the simple title "Father" with which Jesus addresses "Him who sent me" (e.g. Matt. 7 : 21; 10 : 32; John 8 : 26–27; 11 : 41; 12 : 27–28; 17 : 1, etc.). The complete intimacy and trust of this union is awesome and mysterious; the apostles found it so and so do we. We need not be surprised, for this mystery of the triune Divine Being is one which we shall never comprehend. Yet in so far as we *can* comprehend it, we find that it has the elements of trust, love, submission and obedience which are meant to characterise the father–son relationship in earthly families.

The second enrichment is the way in which the Lord Jesus Christ encouraged his disciples to see themselves as penitent believers related to God as children to a Father. He taught us to pray "Our Father . . ." (Matt. 6 : 9) and spoke often to his followers of the loving provision of "Your heavenly Father" (Matt. 5 : 48; Luke 11 : 14). In the Epistles the riches of this theme are further explored – our new birth into the family of God by the sovereign work of the Holy Spirit (John 3) results in children of wrath (Eph. 2 : 3) becoming sons of God by adoption (Gal. 4 : 5–7); heirs of God, and joint-heirs with Christ (Rom. 8 : 17, 1 Pet. 1 : 4). This position of privilege also brings with it the possibility of discipline through the chastisement of suffering and adversity (Heb. 12 : 5–11). But at its heart is a joyful, trusting relationship which allows us to cry "Abba! Father" (Gal. 4 : 6; Rom. 8 : 15). No wonder the Apostle John exclaims: "See what love the Father has given us, that we should be called the children of God; and so we are" (1 John 3 : 1).

To some degree the Christian, like anyone else, will put into the concept of God as Father and into the emotional/attitudinal investment with which such an affirmation is charged, only what he or she has learned from an earthly parent. Words mean what we have learned them to mean, not what a dictionary or theological reference book definition may say they signify. And the title "Father" is an analogy – a taking over – with purification and enrichment – of a universal item in the created order and in human experience.

But in this particular case there are controls and deeper colourings to the analogy. The first and most obvious is the re-promulgation of the duties of fathers and children which Scripture contains, modifying as well as validating the age-old responsibilities of the nuclear kinship relation. In his Appendix to *The Abolition of Man*[34] C. S. Lewis gave illustrations of what he called the Tao, or natural law, from various world religions, showing how Hindu, Babylonian, Egyptian and Greek moral wisdom counselled respect and obedience to parents. So too the Israelite knew he had to honour his father and mother as a basic family duty (Ex. 20). Jesus repeated the commandment (Matt. 19 : 19). Striking or cursing father or mother brought the death penalty in ancient Israel (Ex. 21 : 15, 17; Prov. 20 : 20). Jesus was equally outspoken about those who used a religious technicality to avoid supporting father or mother (Matt. 15 : 1–5 – see also 1 Tim. 5 : 8). The Epistles make obedience to parents the principle duty of children (Eph. 6 : 1–3; Col. 3 : 20), and a test of effective parenthood which is one essential qualification for office in the church (1 Tim. 3 : 4). Yet though tyranny may appear to be only one easy move away from this uncompromising position of obedience, it is beautifully modified by the warning that fathers should not provoke children to anger (Eph. 5 : 4); they are to be positively instructed and fathers are to beware of discouraging them (Col. 3 : 21). It is this degree of discipline which yields good conduct and respect (Heb. 5 : 9,11) of which the Bible speaks, and of wise instruction seasoned with warnings, and illustrations of dangers and disasters, such as we find throughout the book of Proverbs. The practical wisdom of age, with its common-sense summaries of the perennial dangers to life, health and moral integrity – these, says Proverbs, are largely the duty of fathers to transmit. A close-up of the permissive father is only seen once in Scripture. The priest Eli at Shiloh was found wanting in failing to restrain his blashphemous and immoral sons. His protest came too little and too late, and his condemnation was complete and terrible (1 Sam. 3 : 13–14). This then is the pattern of fatherhood in the family which controls and reinforces the instructive insights of most societies. As well as being the Christian model, it also assists in a special way those new Christians who have suffered themselves from distorted or defective parenting, and who for that reason have a particular need to "start from scratch" without a model from their own early experience. In the future such people may constitute more members of our fellowships than we at present envisage. So, by reflex action the divinely-given pattern of father–child relationship purifies and stengthens our concept of our own relation to God as Father.

The second control over the analogy is the Biblical record of God's nature and acts as Father to the redeemed, which we have already outlined. He is the ultimate provider and protector of His people. He is the loving initiator or decider, the trainer or disciplinarian. His overflowing care expresses the goodness of His nature and the firmness of His gracious covenant relationship with His people, whatever may be true of fallible earthly fathers. He is utterly reliable and trustworthy. Though His treatment of His children in specific situations may vary, His basic attitude to us does not. We are part of His family *for good* – in both senses of that phrase.

The third control or influence over our idea of God as Father takes us back into the nature of God Himself, and forms a fitting conclusion. The family pattern persists because it reflects something of the being of God. In a special way fatherhood reflects Him and His nature in a way motherhood cannot. In 1963 C. S. Lewis discerned Robinson's *Honest to God*,[35] with its Germanic "ground-of-being" language, as a cul-de-sac for this very reason. He saw it as a retrograde step towards "Earth-mother" language (which Lewis declared to be less adequate than "Sky-father" language). It is perhaps for this reason too, that Paul on one occasion sharpens the man/woman distinction so much as to assert that man "is the image and glory of God; but woman is the glory of man". Those are Paul's words in 1 Corinthians 11 : 7. The father–husband is the ruler or head, just as Christ is the husband–ruler of the Church (Eph. 5) and of "every man" (1 Cor. 11:3) and as the Father is over the divine Son ("the head of Christ is God" – 1 Cor. 11 : 3).

In this way a fundamental hierarchy is established. An ordering of authority has been declared which stretches right back into the bosom of the Father himself (John 1 :

18). Man and woman enjoy an equality of personal value in the sight of God, but also a difference of function which does imply certain *probabilities* in social leadership roles, and final responsibility and headship to husbands in *all* marriages. This is not to justify male marital tyranny, or decision without discussion, or rule without love. It is to recognise a creation pattern of order – Adam took responsibility *over* woman and *for* her when he named her (as he had the animals) in Genesis 2 : 23. God, who established this dominion by creating Eve after and out of Adam (Gen. 2 : 21) confirmed it after the Fall when he spoke first to Adam as primarily responsible for their common disobedience, though Eve had been the first to sin (Gen. 3 : 6 and 17). The challenge to the Christian husband in Ephesians 5 is to sacrifice for his wife and to give himself as Christ gave himself for the Church. Loving, sacrificial authority is the uniquely Christian contribution to the understanding of how we are meant to see the father in the family.

So fatherhood is fundamental for the family because it is itself in a special way a reflection of the Divine nature – hence the pregnant verse with which we began at the very outset of our examination of relevant material from the Biblical text (in chapter one): "I bow my knees before the Father from whom every family ("patria" with its root in the word for "father") in heaven and earth is named" (Eph. 3 : 15). Man will always gravitate towards the family of patriarchy or male headship, for family and fatherhood in this sense are indivisible in human religious awareness, as are family and motherhood in the biological sense. Ultimately the roots of this knowledge are theological, according to our text. The family with its father-head is in itself a picture in time of one deep and eternal facet of the being of the Creator. In that text "every family" can also be translated "all fatherhood". Is not this ambiguity deliberate?

# CHAPTER FIVE

# Family Decay – Roots and reconstruction

We have now in effect answered the question: Who needs the family? We all do, individually and corporately. Let us first summarise our findings.

We have discovered the massive weight of evidence that points towards the fact that the family, interpreted as a stable, biologically based, two-generational nucleus, with further acknowledged responsibilities to a third generation and usually to a wider kinship network, is indispensable. Though no longer expected in Western society to undertake the manifold tasks which it performs in primitive cultures, the family still forms a focus of mutual affection, understanding, loyalty, care and nurture, both intellectual and emotional, which it is impossible to replicate in any other social structure known to us. Societies which have attempted to dispose of the family have given up the attempt; without renouncing the original concept of the kibbutz, the Israeli scene shows more traditional patterns of husband–wife and parent–child relationship creeping inevitably back. We have seen that every known society regulates the relationship between man and woman as far as children and home are concerned. This man and that woman are bound together, not simply by personal inclination; but additionally and more importantly by some kind of communal mortar, deliberately applied to their union in ritual and regulation and the public proclamation of assumed responsibilities. This is performed regardless of the degree of pre-marital sexual licence which rule or convention may be willing to extend to the sexes at any particular place or period. Cultural energy however seems certainly to vary inversely with the degree of sexual laxity. Unwin has produced massive evidence to support Freud's guess that innovation in art and science and exploration, in the achievement and refinement of a high degree of civilisation, appeared to be linked with strict sexual morality, and in particular with the pattern of pre-marital chastity and monogamous marriage.

Marital stability depends largely upon socially shaped expectations. There is no evidence of instability or widespread neurosis in societies where marriages are arranged, or the choice of spouse severely restricted by law. Thus today's emphasis on personal choice widens the options, but increases the strain of choosing – the self-questioning, the feeling of risk, especially in view of the ambiguity of the concept of love, about which our own culture is so confused with its own failure to distinguish between Venus (carnal desire) and Eros (personal admiration and attraction). The unisex ideal of sexual interchangeability is a denial of the traditional (though often unconscious) model of complementarity, in which each partner contributes a dimension of character, excellence and emotional investment of which the other is constitutionally incapable, or at least far less capable. The marriage of total equality need not deny this polarity of gender differentiation, though even when it acknowledges the different contribution of husband and wife along the expressive – instrumental axis, there is still (if only in practical terms) a need for conflict resolution and thus a need to establish some form of hierarchy. Modern marriage has in some ways a richer potential than marriage according to a more rigid pattern, such as that of Victorian England. But this very fluidity of expectations make it a more risky enterprise for the immature and the less well prepared in terms of economic advantage, intelligence or personality. It is as if the "instruction book" handed to the new aspirant has had so many paragraphs deleted in the past twenty years, that one can scarcely blame the learner drivers for their mistakes in some situations. And remember, we have to imagine a car with dual controls to get the right picture of marriage today. Is it surprising that people feel distinctly unsettled during their early journeys in the vehicle they have just taken over? Yet man and woman still need each other in a deep and exclusive way. The potential of marriage for the healing, growth and support of both partners is better understood today. And there is no possible substitute.

Children still need a mother and a father. Biologically and emotionally mother must be there for survival and healthy development. Many observers believe that hatred of a distinctly female role is endangering the whole idea of motherhood in our own culture and hence disabling tomorrow's mothers from perfoming that most vital of all social tasks. Certainly the career wife – as distinct from the wife with a job (particularly a part-time job) – produces family strains for which increased home affluence cannot fully compensate, and will create a dangerous gap in the child's development during pre-school years. In a different way we saw how children need a father and how societies adopt the principle of legitimacy to ensure as far as possible that every newly arrived member of the community has a male protector and provider. We also noted how father plays a part in assigning status to his children and how his difference of attitude, his frequent absence from home and his traditional function as ultimate focus of discipline, contribute in a special way to the moral development of the child.

Running through all that has been said is the conviction that the family is needed by both the individual and the wider society. Both are threatened if the family disintegrates. Before the rise of sociology, social psychology and psycho-analysis, communities instinctively made provision for strengthening family bonds. In the modern age we understand more of how the family offers its benefits – and alas, how people suffer from the lack of family experience, or from a distorted family experience.

The Christian welcomes this vast new accumulation of data and insight. It is consonant with what he reads in his Bible. At every key point Scripture provides material for the construction of a normative pattern of family relationships – a model stretching back to the structure given at creation, emphasised in the Person and teaching of Jesus, and in some of its fundamental aspects based upon truths concerning God Himself. The Biblical pattern is by no means rigid, as both Old Testament and New Testament make clear. We recall the striking picture of the ideal wife in Proverbs 31. When Jesus achieved our salvation, women were the last at the Cross and the first at the Tomb. In marriage the functions of husband and wife are separate and distinct, yet Scripture allows for role-overlap without role-exchange, or complete fluidity. Motherhood has a special dignity in Christian thinking and fatherhood a peculiar clarity and strength. This normative pattern is written into human nature, so that most societies without revelation have found themselves approximating to it in most respects. The primacy of family loyalties is one of the First Platitudes, as Lewis called them; one of the parts of that Practical Reason which is written on the tablets of the hearts of man, "the sole source of value judgments. If it is rejected, all value itself is rejected."[1]

## I

Today the family in our own society is certainly far from healthy. The only question seems to be: "How sick is it?" Unto death, or only badly ailing? Without answering the question directly, let us examine what is happening to family bonds – those ties that bind men and women in marriage, parents and children in care and respect, and families as micro-communities held together in affection and loyalty.

The symptoms of stress and breakdown are with us on

every side – in the statistics of divorce, separation, desertion, wife battering, child neglect and abuse, children absconding from home and school, and lately of children physically assulting the elderly. At the end of a carefully-staged debate on the family in the House of Lords on May 2nd, 1978, Lord Wells-Pestell for the Government said, amongst other things: "It is really doubtful whether we know enough of what is happening to the family, even to begin to work out a policy for it. We simply do not know what is happening. We do not know what is creating these difficulties; we do not know how to deal with them."[2] These words sound dangerously like the speech of a politician who is abdicating his responsibilities. This profession of humble ignorance is the typical Government answer when the hard statistics of family breakdown and disablement are pressed upon him. The fact that we do not know *everything* about a given problem does not imply that we cannot identify *anything* harmful or put any crooked piece of the picture straight.

In *The Times* of May 20th, 1978 we were told of a divorce granted to the wife of the man who whistled and sang. "Mr. Walter Judge, aged sixty-seven, carried his habit of whistling and singing to such extremes that his wife found it intolerable . . . Mrs. Judge was granted a divorce because the marriage had broken down because of her husband's unreasonable behaviour. Mr Judge, a retired engineer who is still living with his wife in Malting Green, Essex, has denied that the marriage had broken down."[3] Whatever the truth of that particular marriage, the result in the court shows that we have made it easier for men and women to deny the bond of matrimony, to obtain public confirmation that it has broken down beyond repair. There has been a huge increase in such marriage breakdowns. For every two marriages there is one divorce in Britain today. Between 1951 and 1975 the actual number of divorces in England and Wales increased four-fold. And the rate of divorces per thousand marriages increased by only a little under that figure. Children are involved in three out of every four divorces which take place. On average, in every three divorces five children are concerned. Every divorce is a tragedy. Every divorce causes pain, needless pain and often life-long scars. Most divorces involve the suffering of children and most divorces are preventable. Admittedly the modern English divorce law makes provision for reconciliation. But the Bishop of Leicester, speaking in the debate already referred to in the House of Lords, mentioned the reconciliation procedures clause in the Act as "not worth the paper it is printed on" because it is too late. "The only thing that could possibly have prevented the break-up," he continued, "would have been a settled purpose in the minds of both the parties that break-up was unthinkable."[4] When divorces number two and a half thousand per week, we can be sure of one thing. Most need not have happened – either because the marriage could have been saved, or because it ought never to have been contracted. On this scale there is clearly something seriously wrong with marriage and family life in Britain today.

Secondly, with divorce we need to consider wife-battering. This clearly involves almost intolerable strain on a marriage. It is difficult to estimate the real increase in this vicious practice, and reliable figures are very uneasy to obtain. No doubt media coverage, women's rights movements and other factors have contributed to an increased awareness of this type of treatment, which is not the same as demonstrating that there has been absolute increases in its occurrence. But the fact that a nationwide network of hostels is at present being set up, and that the need is so great that many of these hostels fill up swiftly almost as soon as they are opened, seems a clear indication that the general police figures for the increase of violent crime over the last decade must also be reflected in a real increase in the incidence of this particular kind of physical assault.

We turn next to the treatment of children. The same day's edition of *The Times* (May 20th) reports on a sentence of life imprisonment for a man who beat his son to death. "A man who beat to death his quiet and pleasant son aged five was jailed for life by the Central Criminal Court yesterday. The father aged twenty-seven of Brixton was found guilty of the murder of his son Richard last September. Mr. Michael Worsley, for the prosecution, said the boy died from brain injury in horrifying circumstances after being tortured and starved."[5] The rest of the report is almost unbearable to read. Yet we know that this type of incident is not an isolated occurrence. The 1977 Report of the National Society for the Prevention of Cruelty to Children gives figures for child victims of physical abuse in 1976:

> Annually there would be about 7,700 children aged between 0–15 years suspected of being non-accidentally injured in England and Wales. This figure (deliberate infliction of injury) would include 110 fatalities, 1,568 seriously injured children, 5,578 moderately injured children, and 262 children who fail to thrive . . . The number of expected fatalities represents a considerable increase over the NSPCC 1974 register estimate of 27.[6]

These injuries, let it be remembered, are nearly all inflicted by parents. These are the people who brought a child into the world. The NSPCC reports a fourfold increase of deaths from twenty-seven to one hundred and ten in two years. Every three days, it appears from those figures, somewhere in England or Wales, a child dies at its parents' hands. The enormity of this treatment can only be understood as a result of hatred, frustration, and intolerable pressure overriding all the built-in emotions of parental love, rejoicing in the gift of a child, longing to protect the completely dependent and defenceless infant, and the awesome feeling of total responsibility for another little human life. Social workers will know from first-hand experience such homes where feelings do rise to this point. Motherhood is not all sweetness and light. The child who cries incessantly can be a terrible strain on maternal patience and drain all resources of love and sheer physical endurance, especially where no relatives, friends or neighbours can help to relieve the pressure. And an inadequate husband (whether absentee, unsympathetic or just weak) only underlines the bitterness of the mother with a genuinely "difficult" child. Alcohol – a potent factor in many family tragedies – inhibits finer feelings and can make physical assault upon a child more easy to undertake. Yet murder is murder. And whatever pardon individuals may offer to each other, to understand all cannot mean to forgive and forget all in a society which claims to be both humane and just. A society which produces and then excuses such behaviour is in desperate need of Christian understanding and Christian prophecy.

One further factor in parent–child treatment stands out above all others. Once again *The Times* of May 20th reports a hitherto unknown occurrence: Mr. William Paton, a thirty-two-year old Merseyside steel worker was trying by law to prevent his wife destroying their unborn child by abortion. The British Pregnancy Advisory Service is reported as saying: "There is nothing in the Act that allows a husband or boyfriend to have a say in whether a woman goes ahead with an abortion."[7] Mr. Paton, who said he would like to take his case to the House of Lords, is reported to have commented: "I believe that God put us on this earth to create life, not to destroy it." The column also records a statement by the National Abortion Campaign: "The idea that a husband can insist on a woman carrying on with a pregnancy against her will is quite abhorrent. It is the equivalent of slavery. At every turn women find their choice over their own futures, their own bodies and whether or when to have children locked by laws, bureaucracy and a male-dominated medical profession."[8] Without pre-judging either the particular state of the mother's health in this case, or the welfare of her family, or the state of Mr. and Mrs. Paton's marriage (all could be relevant to any judgment of how much support we should offer to any individual in a particular case), it is important to note the language used by the so-called National Abortion Campaign. In fact Mr. Paton failed and his child was destroyed.

Many hospitals now provide what the 1967 Act still specifically forbids – abortion on demand. This particular operation (correctly, if by euphemism, called "termination of pregnancy") happens round the clock at the rate of one termination every five or six minutes in Britain today. As the abortion centre of Western Europe for ten years now – although others are following swiftly in our footsteps as recent events in Italy have shown – we have pioneered legislation to deny human rights to the unborn child and to provide State medical aid to compass its destruction. Hence the situation which is driving so many girls away from or out of the nursing profession, where at one end of the hospital corridor doctors fight to preserve the life of the prematurely born, while at the other end of the same corridor recognisable and often moving and breathing human remains are being removed from the mother and burned. (Many of the allegations in the remarkable book *Babies for Burning*[9] have never been answered or refuted; a carefully-worded apology to one pregnancy advisory service has been agreed in an out-of-court settlement by the authors.) Can the Christian conscience *ever* accept the destruction of infant life on this scale – a scale from which Christians in earlier centuries would have recoiled in horror, and never let their political leaders and opinion-formers rest until it was stopped? Can there be a greater denial of the divine pattern of motherhood than today's "optional motherhood", thanks to the scientific techniques enabling the destruction of the unborn infant?

One-parent families, as they are called now, number over seven hundred and fifty thousand and involve one and a quarter million children. Here again the strain on the individual parent, usually the mother, is obviously greater than it ought to be, and the skewing of the child's development consequently more likely. Yet a recent ITV humorous series[10] presented unmarried motherhood as acceptable, enjoyable and in no way tragic or damaging. Anti-family forces wish us to harden ourselves to an increase of this abnormality too. Here is another aspect of the gradual break-down of family life, and especially of the social consensus in favour of the family ethic. Let us now take the family beyond the two generations. Again on the very same page of *The Times* already quoted we read:

> The mystery of who turned off the life-support machine of Mr. Arthur Davy aged 71, a hospital patient, might never be resolved, it was stated at an inquest in Wolverhampton yesterday. He died after the machine was switched off on New Year's Eve as he lay critically ill in the Royal Hospital, Wolverhampton. The coroner said: "It could have been done intentionally or accidentally, but after investigation it is impossible to establish exactly what happened." He added "In any event death would have occurred very quickly. As I have no evidence to show how it was accelerated I return an open verdict."[11]

What has this to do with family life? The rest of the column makes it plainer.

> Detective Inspector William Squires of the local police said that on New Year's Eve Mr. Davy was deeply unconscious, and his relatives were informed that there was little hope of recovery. His brain, heart and lungs were fading. He was visited by his wife Mary, his bachelor son Jarvis aged forty, and a Mrs. Morris a neighbour. A nurse switched the machine on and connected it to the patient. Mr. Davy was breathing normally as the visitors entered the room. They were left alone in the room for about three or four minutes and the nurse then saw them leave. She told the police that she saw Mrs. Davy at the door of the room, the son at the foot of the bed and the neighbour kissing Mr. Davy. The nurse then took them from the room and was away for about three minutes. When she re-entered the unit she heard the alarm on the machine and found that it had been switched off.[12]

Without wishing to pre-judge this particular case, it raises acutely the problem of our attitude to the elderly and the dependent. We must face the facts which result from having now extended our family concept to three generations. By the mid 1980s there will be more than nine million old aged pensioners in Britain and about seven hundred thousand of them will need some form of daily attention.[13] They form an ever-growing section of the population. Some suffer from dementia – decline in mental functioning with various effects according to the stage of cerebral deterioration. The family is of crucial importance to this particular section of the population. Relatives are often resentful of a burden which they believe should be accepted by society and are unwilling to take responsibility. Few modern houses are large enough to accommodate three generations without friction. Now that more families have become financially dependent on the income of the working wife, and more and more women expect to work either full or part-time once their children have left school, the problems of the aged are acute. The old-fashioned un-married daughter–martyr, who stays at home to look after her parents, seems unlikely to be repeated in future generations. So the family wants to hand responsibility for grandparents over to the State. Now public residential provision is certainly important – *some* strains on *some* families are intolerable. There are ways of making proper provision for one's elderly relatives which do not involve having them in the home. Often the elderly value their in-dependence anyway and prefer to live alone. We show our respect for them by trying to make this possible, and by keeping up regular family visits.

But what if the State cannot provide? Parliament has witnessed constant atheist pressure to legalise euthanasia. There have been three attempts in recent years and there will be more. We should remember certain words because we will certainly hear them again in future years: "burden", "martydom", etc. echoing that word "slavery" applied to motherhood in the context of abortion law debates. Shall we soon hear the slogan "Every Granny a Wanted Granny" used as a support for the next attempt at legalising euthanasia?

The features of family life we have mentioned – divorce, wife-battering, cruelty to children, abortion, propaganda for the destruction of the elderly or infirm – are serious symptoms, and they are increasing. To this survey of symptoms we could add the increase in promiscuous sexual behaviour, both before and after marriage, as evidenced by the dramatic rise in the incidence of sexually transmitted diseases and mirrored – if not promoted – by the magazines for women and teenagers as well in the more obvious propaganda for promiscuity found in the pornographic magazines aimed at men. We must find out next where the attacks on the family comes from.

## II

The first and perhaps most subtle attack of all comes from those we might call "the prophets". Their essays and books do not *appear* to be attacks at all, though they leave the Christian reader vaguely uneasy. They do not assail the family ethic head-on. I am thinking of those persuasive sociologists who blandly extrapolate from present trends. This book relies heavily upon the work of sociologists. It is no part of our intention to devalue their discipline or findings. But extrapolation is a dangerous temptation. In effect, they assert "if things are going in this direction, then they will probably continue going in this direction, and so that's where we're likely to end up". Asked to write on "the family of the future" or "the changing family", they know they must not prescribe. (It is a cardinal sin to tell anyone else what they *ought* to do.) So instead they predict. They very rarely fail to include the most careful qualifications in their introductory paragraphs on the hazardous task of forecasting the future and humble acknowledgments of other possible scenarios. But prophesy they do, and it is the particular picture that they paint, the picture shared by so many of them, which becomes in the end so deeply influential. Thus we have another case of a self-fulfilling prophecy.

One example in our field is the book by Betty Yorburg on *The Changing Family*. This eminent American sociologist writes:

Pre-marital sexual intercourse will be virtually universal for all classes and both sexes, underwritten by developments in medical science and technology, that will almost completely eliminate the danger of unwanted pregnancy . . . The living-together pattern as a prelude to marriage will diffuse from the upper middle-class to other strata and probably become universal in our society . . . The question of power and authority and who has it within the family will become obsolete. The head of the household, as concept and as fact will disappear. Parents will defer and learn from children, if the occasion suggests, as they will defer to and learn from each other.[14]

Another example is found in the last chapter of a stimulating and enjoyable book *People Making*, by an American family therapist, Virginia Satir. But in her last chapter on the family of the future we find her sketching the basic Christian and traditional ethic of the family and then asking, "Why should we accept this as the only possible way?" She suggests various other things that might happen.

What if all the practices now going on, which we have labelled as morally bad, were instead really evidence of the great variations in human beings? In the case of the many-times-married person, perhaps there are some people whose level of interest is short and so they choose one mate after another. Instead of considering this a short-coming, what would happen if we treated this as a simple variation? Such people could enter a limited marriage contract, say from one to five years. If the contract were not renewed at its end, then the dissolution of the marriage could take place. Perhaps the married people who have heterosexual relationships outside marriage are not simply "adulterers", but are people with a human need. After all, polyandry and polygamy were once respected forms of marriage. And why not have a group or communal marriage? When you think about it, marriage merely legalises a relationship between a male and a female adult that entitles them to certain property and a certain guarantee against exploitation. Why does it have to be limited to just one man and one woman? If we fully trusted one another and were truly responsible, we would not be exploitive and we could share fairly.[15]

We may take perhaps just one more example. An excellent symposium of articles on the family by sociologists and social physchologists[16] contains a fascinating last chapter by Suzanne Keller. There can be little doubt of the writer's attitude towards the family as we have described it in our earlier chapters.

It is generally agreed that even in its ideal form the industrial urban family makes great, some would say excessive, demands on its members. For one thing, it rests on the dyadic principle or pair relationship which, as Georg Zimmel observed long ago, is inherently tragic and unstable. Whether in chess, tennis or marriage, two are required to start and continue the game, but only one can destroy it. In this instance moreover, the two are expected to retain their separate identities as male and female, yet be one in flesh and spirit. No wonder that the image of the couple – a major source of confusion and of schism in our society – is highly contradictory, according to whether we think of the sexes as locked in love or in combat. Nor do children, symbols of their union, necessarily unify them. Their own growing pains and cultural demands force them into mutually exclusive socio-sexual identities, thereby increasing the intimate polarity. In fact children arouse parental ambivalence in a number of ways, not least of which is that they demand all and give back too little. And yet their upbringing and sustenance, the moral and emotional climate, as well as the accumulation of econimic and educational resources needed for survival, all rest on this small, fragile, essential, but very limited unit, held together by sentimental rather than by corporate bonds, in which the happiness of the partners is a primary goal, although no-one is very sure what happiness means, nor how it may be achieved and sustained.[17]

Here, with apparent reasonableness, is the case against the family. It is important that it should be put, and that it should be faced. Though man is made for a unique and intimate dyadic relationship, sin has entered the world and its debilitating poison infects every dimension of our experience. Men and women may not only refuse the Biblical roles within the pattern, or even, despite their acceptance, neglect daily repentance and forgiveness within it. They may also reject – or find themselves deprived of – the social support which ideally marriage should always have. Both realism and our own doctrine of sin demand that Christians acknowledge the instability of many (most?) marriages – including those between Christians – yet at the same time not allow the predictions of Keller to be the last word. The God who gave us marriage also gave us the means to painful self-knowledge, to repentance and to forgiveness and restoration. Both individuals and marriages can be *healed*. The Christian offers an alternative future for the family equally valid, yet virtually ignored by the sociological consensus. Perhaps pride of place in popular futurology must go to Alvin Toffler, whose book *Future Shock* (1970) contains most of the ingredients found elsewhere. We may recall he has a chapter called "The Frustrated Family", where he depicts motherhood killed by birth technology and parenthood as a convenient legal and financial arrangement, soon to be despatched. He envisages professional parents who bring up children from many biological sources, and communes of three to six parents, where biological origins would be happily confused. There will be geriatric group families, homosexual family units and so on. The odds, in his view, are very heavily against the monogamous pattern as a provider of fulfilment and satisfaction. Notice the hedonism even in that assumption – that *that* is what it's all about. Toffler sees tailor-made divorce with serial marriage as the new pattern, starting quite naturally with "trial marriage" before anyone under-takes the first proper one. He admits that the stability and sense of continuity awarded by the traditional family pattern of birth, growth, parenthood and fidelity is underminded by this future prediction, but he does not believe that the traditional family can survive.

To the Christian, social prediction is neither sinful nor forbidden. But he sees it as a risky business, and always subject to two powerful provisos. Firstly, the future is logically unpredictable anyway. Every man's free choice is logically unknowable, as Mackay has shown;[18] how much more uncertain is the totality of choices which determine how a society will change and social norms develop. Secondly, the grace of God can powerfully intervene for good; just as the judgment of God can arrive unannounced in social catastrophe through earthquake, flood or crushing defeat in an unexpected war. Or perhaps through a more gradual slide into moral anarchy, barbarism, economic collapse and national decay. Social scientists may be invited to predict. But their forecasts can only be – and must be seen to be – provisional and tentative. The future belongs to

God. Those who offer only *one* future for the family are the most suspect. We must not let them sap our faith or our vision.

The second attack on the family comes from the social engineers. It has been widely recognised that the strong nuclear family encourages the emergence of citizens with a sense of individual worth, a personal feeling of value and identity. Such people represent a potential threat to any large-scale re-shaping of society. Totalitarian regimes have found this in practice. Utopian social engineers from Plato[19] onwards have seen the need to deal with the family in their books and blueprints. For the Utopian totalist state there can only be one focus of emotional attachment and moral obligation. And it must be the same focus for everyone; whether it is the philosopher king or the dictator or the decrees of the party. Any other allegiance is a possible risk to the beauty, harmony and smooth working of the pattern upon which social reconstruction has to be modelled. The well known passage in which Winston Smith, the "hero" of Orwell's *1984*, muses on the way the sex instinct had been canalised and the family subverted in the land of Big Brother, is relevant here.

> How could the fear, the hatred and the lunatic credulity which the party needed in its members be kept at the right pitch except by bottling down some powerful instinct and then using it as a driving force? The sex impulse was dangerous to the party, and the party had turned it to account. They had played a similar trick with the instinct of parenthood. The family could not actually be abolished, and indeed people were encouraged to be fond of their children in almost the old-fashioned way. The children on the other hand were systematically turned against their parents, and taught to spy on them and report their deviations. The family had become in effect an extension of the Thought Police. It was a device by means of which everyone could be surrounded night and day by informers who knew him intimately.[20]

Nazi Germany in the late 1930s displayed this subversion at its worst and Orwell predicts it for a new tailor-made society in *1984*. The sociologists, who have for some time studied tiny utopian mini-communities, as well as totalist dictator-ships which involve a whole nation, have their rather more abstract formulation of how this principle works. And it begins with a paradox. Celibacy and promiscuity, though opposed sexual practices, fulfil an identical sociological function. From a structural point of view they both negate the greatest threat to communal solidarity – a particularis-tic, dyadic attachment. In other words they destroy the unique pair bonding of marriage. The recipe for effective total control is clear. Either no sex anywhere, or sex everywhere. But monogamous fidelity must be stopped.

> Whether members abstain from all sexual relations, as amongst the Shakers, or whether there is Complex Marriage as in Oneida where men and women within the community may and do co-habit for short periods of time, turns out upon inspection to be sociologically un-important. The true enemies of community are those "exclusive and idolatrous attachments" between two persons of opposite sex against which not only Noyes (who founded the Oneida community) but also the Shakers and many others never cease to warn. All utopian communities were concerned with channelling the emotional energies of their members into the brotherhood rather than letting them dribble away into private and exclusive channels.[21]

To bring that right up to the 1970s we need only listen to a voice from the land which has suffered longest and still suffers from the totalist attempt to control individuality. A recent dissident writer in the Soviet Union is Igor Shaverevich, a mathematician and also one of the Helsinki monitors. Looking back at what Marxism has done to his own country, he writes:

> One of the fundamental characteristics of human society is the existence of individual relations between people. As the excellent behaviourist researches of the last decades have shown, we are dealing with a phenomenon of very ancient pre-human origin. There are many kinds of social animals, and the societies they form are of two types: the anonymous and the individualised. In the first (for instance, in a shoal of herrings) the members do not know each other individually, and are interchangeable in their relations. In the second (for example, a gaggle of wild geese) relations arise in which one member plays a special role in the life of another and cannot be

replaced. The presence of such relations is, in a certain sense, the factor which determines individuality. And the destruction of these individual relations is one of the proclaimed goals of socialism – between husbands and wives and between parents and children. It is striking that among the forces which, according to the behaviourists, support these individualised societies we find those of hierarchy and of territory. Likewise in human society hierarchy and property, above all one's own house and plot of land, help to strengthen individuality; they secure the individual's indisputable place in life and create a feeling of independence and personal dignity. And their destruction figures amongst the basic aims advanced by socialism.[22]

The family, it is evident, cannot flourish under a regime that pretends to have infallible or complete knowledge and aspires to total control, even in the best interests of all its citizens. One of the dangers therefore of any shift towards Marxism in any political party or country is precisely this arrogance. The Fascism of Nazi Germany and Mussolini's Italy had its roots in the soil of Marxist socialism, as Hayek has shown in his neglected book *The Road to Serfdom*,[23] which first appeared in 1944, and is now happily not only available again but being read increasingly. So much for the social engineers.

Thirdly, we must note the impact of a group of activists at the political level. It is more difficult to describe clearly their shared characteristics. Their philosophy is a tolerant liberalism, which in the end undermines the family. Many of them are, or have been, our own friends and colleagues. Many have held high political rank in Britain or academic rank in universities. Some of them claim to be Christian. Others are avowed humanists, members of that tiny but influential group of dogmatic atheists, who have been so powerful in the House of Commons (mostly, alas, in the Parliamentary Labour Party) and in the British Broadcasting Corporation over the last twenty years. These are people who appear to have been trying to compensate the population for the increase in state regimentation in every other sphere – taxation, education, trade and industrial legislation and so on – by a corresponding reduction of the legal and conventional curbs on the freedom of entertainers in the matters of language, and humour, publication and stage presentation. In so doing they have largely dissolved the restraints which constitute the morality which supports the family. "Let people say or do what they like as long as no one is obviously hurt" seems to be the principle. It is remarkably reminiscent of the "bread and circuses" argument of the cynical rulers of the ancient Roman Empire in its decadence. In the field of legislation over the past fifteen or twenty years, many people of good will, including some church leaders, have contributed to the easing of legal restrictions in the field of family morality in the mistaken belief that such relaxation would have no effect other than freeing a certain small group of individuals from almost intolerable situations.

A tiny handful of temperamentally abnormal men go in fear of disgrace and blackmail we were told; therefore the law must say nothing about homosexual acts between consenting adults over twenty-one. Parliament and people were assured that nothing else would change if we altered the law. So British law was changed in 1967, and no one can be unaware of the propaganda for the full acceptance of homosexual practices which floods society today. The accusatory procedures of the divorce law, we were told, tends to encourage abuse. The artificial establishment of one guilty party, an unrealistic approach to marital stress, considering individual responsibility or "guilt" on each side separately – all this, we were assured, is very unhealthy, and quite unrealistic. So the law must say nothing of guilt or blame, but allow for an apparently simple item called divorce on grounds of the "irretrievable breakdown" of the marriage. After two years' separation divorce can be granted now by agreement of both parties, after five years it can be granted even if one party registers a refusal. And the result has been a profound change in the concept of marriage. We are now beginning to live with the concept of serial marriage, and the erosion of the Christian ideal of marriage as a life-long commitment. Again, we were told that back-street abortions endangered the lives of perhaps a few thousand girls per year, so we changed the law. The results are appalling. Since the 1967 Abortion Act we have destroyed over one and a quarter million infants in their mothers' wombs in our so-called civilised society. Consider again the so-called "liberation" of writers and dramatists to produce pornography in print, on the screen and on the stage. This is a matter of the highest importance for our cultural life, especially for the male image of woman. Those who engineered the changes in the obscenity law for printed material in 1959, in 1968 for the theatre and the law relating to films in 1977 (this last by a skilful piece of cross-party intrigue at a very late stage of the Criminal Law Bill in the Commons) – all these people knew just what they were doing. They wished to "free" society from what they saw as the dead weight of Christian standards – values such as respect for privacy, the dignity of the individual, the sanctity of marriage – and of course they have let loose the reverse values such as the evils of promiscuity, lust, the destruction of the unborn, disposable marriages, etc.

The studies of the working of pressure groups at Parliamentary level[24] show who these groups were and how they went about their business. There was no widespread demand in the country for any of these legal changes which so deeply affect family ideals. These changes were engineered by a small, dedicated band of humanists, often the same people working under different names. They were often clever enough to enlist ecclesiastical support for their campaigns very early on; the permissive cleric is not a new phenomenon of the 1970s. Often they were able, presumably through Civil Service sympathisers and similar channels, to put arguments into the mouths of Ministers and Departmental spokesmen who should have known better.

Fourthly, we have to confess to Christian ignorance and apathy as a contributary cause of our present plight, though not strictly speaking an "attack". Most Christians, with many other men of good will, were simply unprepared with

Christian affirmations, with facts and with arguments at the crucial moment. As a result they were theologically, legally and sociologically inept or unready to counter the activities of the liberal innovators we have just mentioned. In particular they failed to recognise the declaratory or standard-setting function of the law. As any sociologist will explain, law not only creates or classifies offences and specifies punishments. It also declares the mind of a community about tolerable and intolerable types of behaviour. It thus contributes to social morality as well as reflecting it. To remove a law against a piece of morally reprehensible behaviour may also announce to large sections of the community: "It's now acceptable to behave like that. There's nothing wrong with this kind of activity now." Many citizens, sadly, have little guidance available beyond the law to help them to make moral decisions, especially when they are repeatedly told that divinely-sanctioned morality is either infantile or non-sensical and they are assured that it is an untenable moral position to look to God, Bible or church for sound moral principles. Under these circumstances a law relating to a moral problem becomes of great importance, with or without sanctions. It is significant that Jesus approved of the inclusion of adultery in the Ten Commandments, and indeed deepened its application (Matt. 5 : 27–28), yet apparently refused to press for the correct Old Testament punishment when challenged (John 8 : 1–11). A law is useful even when its sanctions are dormant.

One peculiarly blatant piece of anti-family policy-making by official authorisation is the 1974 circular from the Department of Health and Social Security which appeared to authorise doctors to dispense contraceptives to girls below the age of sixteen (the legal age of consent in this country) without the knowledge of the child's parents or family doctor. The legitimacy of this circular has never been tested in the courts, and there is a very strong case for saying that any doctor so prescribing would be aiding and abetting a criminal offence. But the circular shows how legal or quasi-legal edicts can be a basis for effecting a change in the moral climate, and for shifting the ethical footholds of the medical profession. A good case could be made for believing that such official pronouncements are quite consciously paving the way for a reduction of the legal age of consent as "unrealistic" or "impracticable". There has been considerable – but ineffective – public protest recently at the intention of the Doncaster Area Health Authority to set up, on the basis of this circular, a sex clinic for young people which will dispense contraceptives to girls as young as eleven and twelve without parental knowledge and without informing the child's general practitioner.[25] This is a very good example, both of the way the moral climate can be altered by official (in this case not even Parliamentary) memorandum, and of Christian unpreparedness – only one secular body (the Responsible Society) and one or two inter-denominational Christian organisations (principally the Festival of Light) took up this issue. Official church sources, spokesmen and committees either did not know or did not care.

From "liberal" politicians and unready Christians we turn fifthly to commercial interests. Many have guessed at some links between those people active politically to loosen restraints upon anti-family behaviour, and those who stand to profit from increased sales of contraceptives, of pornographic material, or the increased use of places in private abortion clinics, for example. Such direct links are very hard indeed to establish, at any rate with the firmness that would stand up to any statement in a court of law. But once an immoral entrepreneur sees a future in exploiting any field open to him for financial gain, he will do so. From the monopoly contraceptive industry to Mr. Paul Raymond's five and a half million pound empire of London sex theatres and so-called "men's magazines", we can see the money being made from sexual indulgence. Commercial interests are not going to ask whether their activities present an image of woman as nothing but a thrill-machine for men, an object of male lust. Nor are contraceptive manufacturers going to take steps to see that their products are only used by married couples when the main aim is to maximise profits. The commercial advantages of the family-splitting youth culture too, all the paraphenalia of jeans, pop music ("the charts", records, guitars, posters etc.) and specialist magazines has also been fully exploited in the last fifteen years, and has to a very large degree divided the generations further by creating the self-conscious teenage consumer class, as Oxford sociologist Bryan Wilson has pointed out.[26]

The sixth source of anti-family influence is the mass media. One particular seven-day sensation during 1978 is symbolic of a new mass interest sedulously fostered for more than a decade by an increasing number of newspapers. In May 1978 every newspaper featured prominently the dispute about who was to be allowed to publish the memoirs of Miss Joyce McKinney.[27] Miss Joyce McKinney is a Mormon (or ex-Mormon) beauty queen who was alleged to have abducted and held captive a male Mormon missionary. At her earlier court appearance, before she jumped bail and fled to the United States, her case featured prominently in *The Times*. Descriptions of sexual activity in which she was alleged to have participated were given in such detail as I have never previously met in the columns of *The Times*. But *The Times* was only following the trend of sexual explicitness carved out by pornographic magazines first, then by women's magazines in the middle '70s. An obsessive and prurient interest in sexual activity, voluntary or forced, normal or deviant, erodes the private realm, encourages a mechanical and hedonistic view of human relations and crushes both civilised reticence and respect between the sexes. Such an interest is however comparatively easy to kindle and to feed, especially in the male half of society. The massive circulation of newspapers and magazines catering for this taste shows it to be an addiction. Pornographic cinemas exist in all large cities. Television is increasingly explicit. There can be little doubt that this change in entertainment and in attitudes does not help the family. Divorce lawyers are increasingly testifying to the breakdown of husband/wife relationships as a result of male addiction to pornography. The mass media have much to answer for, and their insensitivity to individuals and groups calling for higher standards is serious. Most academic psychologists and sociologists have also been strangely reticent. A welcome change should however be noted; Professor Hans Eysenck's most recent book is quite unambiguous on the impact of the mass media upon attitudes and behaviour, and calls for action.[28]

All these groups, then, have conspired, sometimes consciously, sometimes unconsciously, to erode the beauty and dignity of the man/woman marriage relationship. With their associated groups of militant feminists (virtually all atheists) they have bitterly attacked the female/male polarity; they have attempted to split child-bearing from marriage and parents from children. Human life, especially infant life is becoming disposable. Marriage is becoming disposable. The anti-family movement, with all its manifold pressures, is to a large degree guided by the ethic of human and family disposability.

### III

How can we envisage the task of Christian witness and Christian reconstruction amid so many hostile influences?

There must firstly be *a renewed grip on Scripture at every level in our churches.* There was never a greater need for Bible preaching, Bible teaching and group Bible study. As individuals and as churches corporately we need to be recalled to the firm and unchanging standards of God's Word. This is the way of life, health and peace. Here is no cramping uniformity, but rather a generous variety of possible variations within the permitted pattern through which the family can grow and develop, given the basic principles which Scripture outlines. But Christians must know what the principles are, speak of them plainly and without shame, and determine that they will never abandon them. How many Christians would recognise the inadequacy of the definition of the family offered by a sociologist at the opening session of a recent conference: "A small group of people in which one or more adults are caring for one or more dependent children"? And how many would rise and oppose it in Christ's name? (No-one did.) And Christians must strive to re-impregnate the whole of society with this awareness of what God demands and how wise and health-giving His provisions are. An Old Testament scholar has pointed out recently how many devices we find in ancient Israel for encouraging observance of the law, in particular through festivals and through the activities of the Levites – who thus "played a role equivalent to the mass media in modern society"![29] Certainly school religious education has some significance in this respect too.

This renewed grip on Scripture – perhaps, more correctly, Scripture's renewed grip upon us – must then be lived out in Christian families. Any kind of counter-attack or attempt to halt anti-family influences will surely fail to be credible unless we have Christian families and homes which are radiating Gospel light and love, showing that God's way *works*, and that people are happier within the order of Scripture than they are with all the permissive or destructive alternatives increasingly on offer in society around. And there is room for considerable self-examination amongst ourselves. As we allow Scripture to grip us once more, we must ask ourselves at all points whether we have not, even within our own Bible-believing, evangelical tradition, allowed certain things to creep in which are foreign to these principles.

It is fashionable to deplore the Victorian age. Christians will not join in the sneering, for they know how greatly God blessed our nation spiritually as well as economically in the nineteenth century. Yet not all was pure gain. Are some of us still acting with Victorian rigidity? Early twentieth-century evangelical households often suffered from a crippling form of paternal authority which did not permit much personal growth to wives or children. Again, until recently most evangelical Christians have been more mealy-mouthed than the Bible itself about certain human sins. Some Christian people are still deeply suspicious of a Bible-based social witness like that of the Festival of Light for the very reason that it speaks frankly of human sin. Again, how is it that the evangelical world seems to foster a tendency to develop the militaristic woman – the "evangelical boss-cat" as she has been named? Some of our most distinguished evangelical Christian households over the last twenty or thirty years have thrown up this particular type of woman with disturbing regularity. The reverse aspect of this strange development is seen in the male side of the Christian partnership. One hears many Christian young women saying to their friends from time to time: "How is it that there are so few Christian *men* around the place?" By this they simply mean men who can be admired for their properly masculine qualities – initiative, strength, tender protective-ness (which is courtesy) towards women and children, disciplined and willing to discipline others, with a capacity to take responsibility and to make decisions and a clear ambition towards personal and spiritual maturity. There will always be a wide range of personality types in the church, as there are in the world. But Christian maturity will challenge men to become more like the Biblical husband and father, just as women will be called to become more truly women. The androgynous human is no part of God's design, nor is the unisex culture. A renewed grip on Scripture and Scripture's renewed grip upon us will give us a true vision so that we can correct such frustrating tendencies.

Secondly we need *a renewed sensitivity to the attacks on the family*, the distortion of the family pattern, the challenges to the family, and the various influences which make for the erosion of the family ethic. We must do our homework. The Festival of Light is a service organisation dedicated to the continued attempt to isolate or identify these forces, to document their activities, to supply a Christian (i.e. Scriptural) evaluation and to lay them before Christian people, so that the churches can be aware of what is going on and how to work for healthy change. Enough has been said earlier in this chapter to underline this need for vigilance and understanding here.

We can only point out that the Government must be pressed by every legitimate means to consider all new legislation in the light of its possible impact upon the family. And if existing legislation is inadequate to protect the family, to foster family values (in so far as law *can* do this – there are naturally limits in a democracy) and to penalise family wreckers – then the law must be strengthened. A number of important ways in which Government action or inaction *can* affect the health of the family were mentioned by speakers in the two House of Lords debates on June 16th, 1976 and May 2nd, 1978.[30] These debates will repay careful study.

The most recent Church of England Report on the subject, *Marriage and The Church's Task* (C.I.O., 1978, p. 69) has no doubt about the importance of positive national policies. It states quite categorically: "there is a curious discrepancy at the level of public policy-making, between an increasing awareness of the need for concerted policies for the family, and an almost total lack of interest in sustaining marriages. With the possible exception of the limited public funds channelled to marriage counselling agencies, there is next to no sign that Government values marriage as an important social institution. This cannot but have an impact in time on general public attitudes and on the expectations with which particular couples enter upon marriage. It must indeed be said that there is a lack of consistency between policies bearing on family life. We urge the need for intensive study within Government, whether by existing Departments, the Central Policy Review Staff or by a new agency acting as a centre of advocacy for marriage and family affairs, of the impact of government policies on married couples and families, who make an indispensable contribution to social well-being."

Thirdly, *we need repentance and a renewed openness to correction in our own families and churches.* Many Christian families today bear no distinctive marks of their Christian profession. For example, what has happened to family prayers – to Bible reading and prayer led by father at the breakfast table, and/or after the evening meal? Is life *so* different from that of our Christian forbears that such family worship is now either impossible or unnecessary? Yet it is certainly less frequent. Again, our own Christian families have been less open than they should be, less "extended" than they would have been if we had discerned the Bible pattern. Should we take more seriously the three-generation family pattern rather than two-generation norm which economic and occupational developments have forced upon us? And if the answer comes that houses make it impossible, living conditions don't allow for it, then perhaps we ought to ask our planners, builders and local authorities (and even governmental advice) to change the kind of houses which are being built. What of the openness of the Christian family to hospitality? Both occasional and residential hospitality is clearly encouraged in Scripture. Are Christian households distinguished by the welcome they offer to the newcomer, the bachelor, the new church member, the immigrant, the single school mistress or social worker living alone, the student, the man just out of prison . . . and so on? Are we "given to hospitality" (Heb. 13 : 1–2) as we should be? An interesting observation in the experience of many has been the recent decline in simple hospitality over a meal which Christians can offer to each other. Yet there is something precious, symbolic and greatly sustaining in eating together. When grace is said before *that* meal, it can be felt to be so much more of a real blessing. We are all so busy. If we are all so busy as not to be able to break bread together in our homes in Christian fellowship, so that friendship and trust can develop, and sharing of joys and sorrows as a consequence, then perhaps there is something wrong with the pattern of our family lives. Hospitality can – and in a minority of households has – undercut the proper amount of care and attention due to children. But today observation suggests that this risk of excessive hospitality is rarely incurred.

A renewed openness to correction is needed in the inner dimensions of family life too. Many Christian marriages are blighted – apparently beyond repair in some cases – by subtle forms of selfishness. Burdens are not shared, resentments not expressed, sullen separations never bridged, attempts not made *together* to understand each other's needs, misunderstandings, aspirations, expectations of marriage, silent disappointments and so on. It is worth recalling that so much "secular" marriage counselling is simply a name for helping a couple just to talk sensitively to each other about their own feelings (often for the first time).

It needs to be affirmed loudly and clearly that God the Holy Spirit can and does restore marriages, or make them "work" for the first time after years of quiet dissatisfaction. Though He is able to do this by working directly upon the minds and hearts of one or both partners as they pray, read the Bible and examine their own hearts, more often there will be a social dimension to such healing. Indeed, what more natural than that these readjustments should take place in the setting of Christian fellowship, with one part of the Body of Christ ministering to another? Older Christian couples have a great responsibility here if their marriage is by God's grace a healing, caring and supporting relationship in which the exchanges of love are positive and enriching, and the home is a place of warmth and understanding. Why should not every local church or fellowship set aside one or two couples to undertake this ministry within the body of believers locally? Prayer, reading and perhaps some more formal "training" would add to the value of their ministry, which might also extend to the engaged and the newly-married.

In such counselling situations the highest standards of confidentiality would of course be adopted, such as would pertain in seeking medical advice. If the advice columns of women's magazines are any indication, many difficulties are comparatively simple to grasp and to deal with, provided anonymity can be assured. This requirement might mean that one pair of Christian marriage advisers might function better in ministering in a neighbouring or associated fellowship rather than in their own church. They would soon be needed outside the church too. In a remarkable article in the *Sunday Telegraph* recently (April 10th, 1977) Allen Andrews boldly affirmed that the Christian churches were uniquely qualified with both the knowledge and the resources to save marriage and the family for the whole nation. Does the salt retain enough of its savour for us to rise to this friendly challenge?

The life of every Christian family should interact with the life of the local church to the enrichment of both. This means, for example, that any special time of stress (bereavement, separation, financial or occupational disaster, etc.) will immediately be more widely known and resources for support will be available at once from the total family network which forms the local church. If the local church consists of people of all ages at various stages of personal and spiritual development and with a wide variety of life-experiences, social and intellectual as well as spiritual, then there will be a multiplicity of resources upon which the individual family can call in times of difficulty. And there will even be sensitive individuals (in addition to the pastor himself) who may become aware of developing strains before a family itself realises what is happening.

A local church fosters this kind of life by being careful only to segregate members by sex and by age when there is a very strong reason for such a division. Normally, therefore, meetings for prayer, Bible study etc. should allow all to contribute what they can (including questions) above the age of early childhood. Restricted gatherings need special justification.

Nothing teaches behaviour and communicates moral standards more effectively than a good model. If our own Christian homes and families radiate contentment, security, warm acceptance and understanding, and are *felt* as places of blessing and health, we shall be commending the Gospel and providing our children – and the young people of the surrounding neighbourhood – with an argument for God's family pattern which cannot be gainsaid. So many youngsters today are without positive models. If Christian family life is in good repair, we shall have models as well as words of advice to counter contemporary confusion.

Fourthly and finally, *we need a renewed vision of the spiritual battle* which is at present taking place. Any attack on the family is an attack upon God Himself, because the Scriptural pattern of family relationships is a given, divine ordinance. It is not just a structure which man has discovered by accident or thought up for himself, but something which God wants men and women to have for their own happiness and fulfilment. God gives us a clear family pattern because He has designed us with this in mind. Family order is for His glory and our good. So there can be no doubt where the attacks on the family ultimately come from. Promises of "liberation" from family obligations come from the father of lies himself. Satan often uses ignorant, and sometimes pleasant and well-meaning people, to try to achieve what he wishes. The demonic control of the unconverted – including psychiatrists and sociologists who are not believers – is a truth not heard frequently today. Often such men are assisted by the "common grace" of God, and write or speak words of truth and positive worth. In those cases they rise above the spiritual sphere to which they properly and personally belong (Eph. 2 : 1–3). At other times the same writers will be hostile to Scripture and cleverly destructive. We have been warned.

The attacks today are upon Christian individuals and upon Christian families, as well as upon whole churches and nations. It is said that many more divorces are taking place today amongst believing Christian people than ever before. Certainly those nations which have traditionally called themselves "Christian" (our own in particular) seem to have been under an unparalleled attack as far as the family is concerned.

What is the secret of renewal in this sphere? I believe that British social life is at the cross-roads. We have now reached the point where over wide areas of our society there is simply no Christian witness at all, not even (as far as one can see) one Christian making personal human contact with communities of hundreds, if not thousands. The mass media cannot or will not bring them Christian truth. It is no surprise that family structures crumble. Now one thing only can save the family for our nation. There is only one power which will put the Divine pattern back into the family, though there may be a grim alternative of sorts. Admittedly, a take-over by some sort of totalitarian government could bring us to our senses. It has done in more than one other society. Few would want Britain to go that way however, because of what happens to human freedom and dignity under those conditions. But there is another way. There is only one force that can cleanse, heal and restore family order and keep us free at the same time, and that is an old-fashioned Gospel revival. I have never been the same since my reading of *England Before and After Wesley* by J. W. Bready[31] many years ago. That vivid scholarly history of the social impact of the eighteenth-century Evangelical Revival shows beyond any doubt that every aspect of social life, including family life, can be transformed by a preaching of the Gospel up and down this country like that of George Whitfield and John Wesley, preaching which brought men and women back to God through deep repentance and faith in Jesus Christ.

Many secular observers, dramatists and novelists, speak

today of people living a harsh and brutal life without hope. Such was the life of the many thousands who heard Wesley and Whitfield in the "gin age" – the age of Hogarth and of elegant atheism. What better or more wonderful hope can there be than that given in the Gospel of Christ? What else can give a sense of worth and identity to a man or a woman in a godless culture? What more amazing affirmation of my individuality than to hear for the first time that Christ died for my sins? That is how God loves *me*. If that message can come back to Britain in and through our churches, I believe we shall have taken the crucial turn towards the national restoration of family life. Does prayer for nationwide revival feature reguarly in our private and public prayers? We have heard much of "evangelism" and "mission" of late in almost all ecclesiastical circles. "Renewal" too is a fashionable if somewhat fluid concept. It might be more profitable if we were to be quite specific and urgent in our prayers for the conversion of England, for deep repentance in the church, for the power of the Spirit behind faithful preaching of the whole Gospel, and for a sense the majesty, the love and the wrath of God throughout the land. The Holy Spirit would restore families as well as cleanse and renew individuals in a revival of this depth and extent.

What should be our attitude until this happens? Perhaps the attitude of the faithful Christian pilgrim is best expressed by some words not from the Bible, but from a work of fiction by a Christian writer of our own time.

"Always after a defeat and a respite, the Shadow takes another shape and grows again."

"I wish it need not have happened in my time," said Frodo.

"So do I," said Gandalf, "and so do all who live to see such times. But that is not for them to decide. All we have to decide is what to do with the time that is given to us."[32]

# Notes

*Chapter 1*

1. H. Belloc, *Cautionary Verses* (Duckworth, 1940, etc.) p. 98.
2. E. A. Nida, *Culture, Customs and Christianity* (Tyndale, 1963) pp. 97–99.
3. In *The Family in Society: Dimensions of Parenthood* (HMSO, 1974) p. 12.
4. *The Changing Family* (Columbia U.P., 1973) p. 110.
5. Penguin, 1973 (3rd edn.).
6. *The Family in Society: Dimensions of Parenthood* (HMSO, 1974) pp. 91–92.
7. *What Freud Really Said* (Penguin, 1967) p. 184.
8. In *Social Work Today*, July 15th, 1971 issue, p. 5.
9. D. Cooper, *The Grammar of Living* (Penguin, 1974) p. 14.
10. D. Martin, *Tracts Against the Times* (Lutterworth, 1973) p. 98.
11. K. Marx and F. Engels, *The Communist Manifesto* (C. P. Centenary Edition, 1948) pp. 16–17.
12. F. Engels, *Origins of the Family, Private Property and the State*, quoted in Bell and Vogel (ed.), *A Modern Introduction to the Family* (Free Press, 1960) p. 53.
13. Bell and Vogel (ed.), op. cit. p. 58. See also R. L. Coser and L. A. Coser in R. L. Coser (ed.) *The Family: its structures and functions* (Macmillan, 1974) pp. 99–102.
    See also N. S. Timasheff, *The Great Retreat* (Dutton, N.Y., 1946) and P. Sorokin, *The American Sex Revolution* (Porter Sargent, USA, 1957).
14. ibid. p. 60.
15. e.g. M. E. Spiro in Bell and Vogel (ed.), op. cit. pp. 64–75, also Yonina Talmon, 'The Family in a Revolutionary Movement – the Case of the Kibbutz in Israel' in R. L. Coser (ed.), op. cit. pp. 550–578. See also the problems of the first generation of aged kibbutz-dwellers noted in *The Times*, September 12th, 1978 issue, p. 18.
16. Y. Talmon in R. L. Coser (ed.), op. cit. p. 562.

17. C. S. Lewis, *The Abolition of Man* (O.U.P., 1943; Bles 1946; Macmillan, N.Y., 1947).
18. See *The New Bible Dictionary* (IVP, 1962) p. 417
19. In *Vocabulary of the Bible* (Lutterworth, 1958), s.v. 'Family'.
20. Quoted in J. Poulton, *Dear Archbishop* (Hodder & Stoughton, 1976) p. 19.


*Chapter 2*
1. G. Murdock, *Social Structures* (N.Y., 1949).
2. Quoted in Bell and Vogel (ed.), *The Family* (Free Press, 1960) p. 47.
3. In R. L. Coser (ed.), op. cit. p. 29.
4. ibid. See also Lingsely Davis, *Human Society* (Macmillan, N.Y., 1949) for an important discussion of the incest taboo.
5. J. D. Unwin, *Sex and Culture* (O.U.P., 1934) p. viii.
6. ibid, pp. 618–9.
7. ibid, p. 23.
8. ibid, p. 340.
9. ibid, p. 414.
10. ibid, p. 431.
11. Huxley in *End and Means* (Chatto and Windus, 1965) and D. Mace quoted in V. Packard, *The Sexual Wilderness* (Pocket Books, N.Y., 1970).
12. Yorburg, op. cit. p. 18.
13. ibid. p. 197.
14. C. S. Lewis, *The Four Loves* (Bles, 1960, Fontana, 1963) pp. 86, 88.
15. ibid. pp. 87–88.
16. ibid. p. 86.
17. In R. L. Coser (ed.), op. cit. p. 140.
18. ibid. p. 111 ff.
19. "Marriage and the construction of Reality: an essay in the microsociology of knowledge" in R. L. Coser (ed.), op. cit. pp. 157–174.
20. ibid. p. 159.
21. See, for example, his *Christian Marriage* (Darton, Longman and Todd, 1965), *Marital Breakdown* (Penguin, 1968) and *The Marriage Relationship Today* (Mothers Union, 1974).
22. See D. Field, *The Homosexual Way – A Christian Option?* (Grove Books, 1975). There can be no doubt that the Bible excludes homosexual genital practices as an option for any believer; such activity is inevitably included in any Scriptural definition of sin.

23. "In ancient Israel, religious offences and offences against life
    and the structure of the family tended to be punished more
    severely than elsewhere; whereas cuneiform law tended to
    rate financial loss as more serious than loss of life." – G.
    Wenham in *Law Morality and the Bible*, ed. Kaye and
    Wenham (IVP, 1978) p. 39. See also pp. 34–37 (on the seventh
    commandment) and 42–43 (on the death penalty). A number
    of the other essays are very relevant to the theme of this
    book.

*Chapter 3*

1. Penguin edition (1964) p. 10.
2. *One Flesh* (Grove Books, 1975) p. 4.
3. ibid. p. 10.
4. In Bell and Vogel (ed.), op. cit. pp. 333–334.
5. In R. L. Coser (ed.), op. cit. p. 53.
6. ibid. p. 56.
7. ibid. pp. 57, 58.
8. Hansard (Lords) Vol. 391, no. 70, col. 53.
9. R. Hoggart, *The Uses of Literacy* (Penguin, 1958) pp. 27–37.
10. G. F. Gilder, *Sexual Suicide* (Millington, 1974) pp. 244–246.
    This powerful analysis has been unjustly neglected, notwith-
    standing a tendency to overstatement.
11. Coser, op. cit. p. 23.
12. Hansard, op. cit., col. 89.
13. Winnicot, op. cit. p. 17.
14. ibid. p. 30.
15. J. Bowlby, *Child Care and the Growth of Love* (Penguin,
    1953) p. 78.
16. Penguin, 1972, esp. p. 20.
17. ibid. p. 30.
18. *Women and Holy Orders* (C.I.O., 1966) p. 67.
19. ibid. p. 67.
20. For a fuller discussion from a Biblical point of view see V.
    Subilia, *The Problem of Catholicism* (E.T., SCM, 1964) pp.
    42–45, and G. C. Berkouwer, *The Conflict with Rome* (E.T.,
    Presbyterian and Reformed Publishing Co., Philadelphia,
    1958) ch. 6.
21. *The Guardian,* May 2nd, 1978 issue, p. 9.
22. In *Obeying Christ in a Changing World*, Vol. 3, ed. Kaye
    (Collins, 1977) p. 112.
23. A point made by O'Donovan in an earlier (unpublished) ver-
    sion of his paper in the symposium mentioned in note 22
    above. The medical correspondent of *The Times* notes the

statistics of present behaviour in the Western world in the issue of July 19th, 1978 under the heading "Children are going out of style"; more than half the children of Britain come from one or two-child families and fewer women are marrying; delayed marriage and extra-marital co-habitation are becoming more frequent, and we may well soon be in a position position where a third of women never have children. It would then be unlikely that the birth-rate would reach replacement level.

*Chapter 4*
1. In Bell and Vogel (ed.), op. cit. p. 261.
2. ibid. p. 21.
3. ibid. p. 399.
4. In R. L. Coser (ed.), op. cit. pp. 58–59.
5. ibid. p. xviii.
6. ibid. p. 94 ff.
7. ibid. p. 248.
8. In Bell and Vogel (ed.), op. cit. p. 334.
9. In *Social Work Today,* July 15th, 1971 issue, p. 6.
10. In Bell and Vogel (ed.), op. cit. p. 350.
11. p. 115.
12. L. Eickhoff in *Education: Threatened Standards*, ed. R. Boyson (Churchill, 1972) pp. 36–37.
13. See D. Stafford-Clark, op. cit. pp. 167–168.
14. *Bringing Up Children in a Difficult World* (Bodley Head, 1974) p. 247.
15. ibid. p. 248.
16. Bell and Vogel (ed.), op. cit. p. 536
17. ibid. p. 248.
18. Eickhoff, op. cit. pp. 37–38.
19. In Bell and Vogel (ed.), op. cit. pp. 499–509.
20. ibid. p. 272.
21. idem.
22. In Bell and Vogel (ed.), op. cit. p. 528.
23. Penguin, 1957.
24. In *The Family in Society: Dimensions of Parenthood* (HMSO, 1974) p. 33.
25. ibid. p. 34.
26. In Bell and Vogel (ed.), op. cit. p. 117.
27. February 1946 issue, reprinted in Bell and Vogel (ed.), op. cit.
28. ibid. p. 566.
29. *Women and Holy Orders* (C.I.O., 1966) p. 64.
30. In *The World's Religions* (IVP, 1st edn. 1950) p. 92.

31. R. Brow, *Religion: Origins and Ideas* (Tyndale, 1966) p. 14.
32. op. cit. pp. 101–02.
33. *Calvin's Doctrine of Man* (Lutterworth, 1959) p. 43.
34. *The Abolition of Man* (Macmillan edn., USA, 1959) p. 43. See also S. Greengus, "Law in the Old Testament" in *The Interpreter's Dictionary of the Bible* (Abingdon, N.Y., 1977) pp. 532–537.
35. "Must Our Image of God go?", reprinted in *Undeceptions* (Bles, 1971) pp. 149–150.

*Chapter 5*
1. C. S. Lewis, *The Abolition of Man* (Macmillan edn. USA, 1965) p. 56.
2. Hansard (Lords), Vol. 391, No. 70, col. 114.
3. *The Times*, May 20th, 1978 issue, p. 3.
4. Hansard, op. cit. col. 55.
5. *The Times*, loc. cit.
6. *Child Victims of Physical Abuse* (N.S.P.C.C., n.d. [1978]) p. 5.
7. *The Times*, loc. cit.
8. ibid.
9. Serpentine Press, 1974. The book is at present out of print in the UK though translations have been published in other European languages. A number of legal actions relating to the contents of the book have failed to invalidate the substantial accuracy of the book's main thrust.
10. *Miss Jones and Son*, starring Paula Wilcox.
11. *The Times*, loc. cit.
12. idem.
13. Dr. Tony Smith in *The Times*, February 21st, 1978 issue.
14. B. Yorburg, op. cit. pp. 198–200.
15. V. Satir, pp. 298–299.
16. *The Family: Its Structures and Functions*, ed. R. L. Coser (Macmillan, 1974).
17. ibid. p. 583.
18. In, for example, *Christianity in a Mechanistic Universe* (IVP, 1965) p. 51 ff.
19. Plato, *The Republic*, trans. F. M. Cornford (Oxford, 1941) pp. 152–164.
20. G. Orwell, *1984* (Penguin, 1954) pp. 109–110.
21. L. A. Coser, "The Sexual Requisites of Utopia" in R. L. Coser (ed.), op. cit. p. 534,
22. In A. Solzhenitsyn (ed.), *From Under the Rubble* (Fontana, 1976 edn.) p. 58.

23. Routledge 1944 and 1966.
24. See, for example, P. Richards, *Parliament and Conscience* (Allen and Unwin, 1970), B. Pym, *Pressure Groups and the Permissive Society* (David and Charles, 1974), and the bibliographies therein.
25. See the *Daily Telegraph,* April 27th, 1978, the editorial "Degrading" and the report of a public meeting in Doncaster; also *Daily Express* editorial January 27th, 1978.
26. B. Wilson, *Youth Culture and the Universities* (Faber and Faber, 1970), passim.
27. e.g. *The Times*, May 20th, 1978.
28. H. J. Eysenck and D. K. B. Nias, *Sex, Violence and the Media* (Temple Smith, 1978), esp. ch. 11 (p. 253 ff.).
29. G. Wenham in *Law Morality and the Bible* (IVP, 1978) p. 45.
30. Hansard (Lords), Vol. 371, No. 87 and Vol. 391, No. 70.
31. Hodder and Stoughton, 1938 – now, alas, out of print.
32. J. R. R. Tolkien, *The Lord of the Rings* (Allen and Unwin, 1954), Vol. 1, p. 60.